How to Carve a
Pineapple

Things we learned and loved on
our adventure around the world

SHAUNA DESMARAIS

Danica SM Ann

tellwell 🖋

Tellwell Talent
www.tellwell.ca

ISBN
978-0-2288-4213-2 (Paperback)
978-0-2288-4214-9 (eBook)

CONTENTS

ACKNOWLEDGEMENTS

First and foremost thanks goes to my Lord and Saviour Jesus Christ. I was introduced to him at an early age and have walked closely with him ever since. He has been forever faithful. I cherish my relationship with him deeply and the gift and passion for writing that he blessed and trusted me with.

Thanks to my ever patient hubby and kids. They oblige my crazy, outlandish ideas, my never ending need for space and alone time and my endless pursuit of where to next! They know me better than anyone and still graciously and unconditionally love me.

Thanks is most certainly due to my parents for their endless support. Whether it's a move, a trip around the world or a new business or job, I can always rely on their enthusiasm and excitement. They are a soft place to fall in a hard world.

Thanks to my bestie and fellow writer Tan for all the late night phone calls, the help brainstorming a title and the constant camaraderie. We share a passion for faith, travel and the pursuit of the next grand adventure. Life has taken us each around the world and we always end up closer than before. I deeply value our relationship.

Thank you to my editor and old friend Danica. She was on speed dial (text) many times and was both encouraging and honest, which I badly needed. I wrote this book, she refined it. I believe it was good and she made it great. I am so grateful to have had the privilege to reconnect and have the opportunity to work together.

Last but not least, many thanks goes to my family and our forever friends. There are many. They shared in our excitement as we prepared for our trip, covered us in prayer and encouragement along the way, listened to my endless ramblings and understood my sorrow with returning home. I always knew we had a community to return to, regardless of where life took us.

Dear Reader,

This is my story. I knew long before we even left on our trip that I would be writing a memoir about it. I had started blogging years before and much to my shock and awe, people loved reading it. This was great news as I LOVED writing it. The bad news was, I hated the attention I got from it and was always one negative comment away from never writing again (which thankfully never happened.) It became an avenue to share personal stories from our home life and homeschooling, a place to share my thoughts regarding faith and marriage and parenting and of course my love of travel and adventure! So it was fitting that as we began the journey to plan and prepare for our big adventure, I blogged about it all, before, during and after. These are the entries that you will see before most chapters. My idea (against the possibly better judgement of my editor) was that you would hear me from a different point of view. The blog posts are me, where I was at the time, how I was feeling and snippets of our adventures in real time. The actual chapters that follow are much the same but are also in addition, where I dig in and go into great depth after years of reflection and thought. If you find the posts too repetitive, just skip them! I will not be offended (and of course I'll never know).

Because this is a memoir and I'm doing the writing, it is written from my point of view. Many times over the years, I have jogged each of our memories for city names and locations, restaurants, conversations and special events. My family is well aware that I am open and honest about how things went from my perspective, which is also my reality. They may have had vastly different experiences and they were given many opportunities to read along as I wrote and potentially offer their perspective, to which no one really obliged. So to them I say… No complaining!

All of the stories I tell are 100% truthful from my perspective but I did take care to ask anyone and everyone involved if they gave me their permission to have their real names included. With the exception of one couple, all names and their relationships to us are real and factual. As I've gotten older my short term memory and extended long term memory is getting terrible. It is amazing to me however, that the details (big and small) of this time period are seared into my memory. I can easily recall arrivals, departures, flights, road trips, people, conversations, food that we ate and in lots of cases what day of the week it was. This just shows you how life-changing, stretching, and memorable it was. It is truly something none of us will ever forget. I hope and pray you love it as much as I have loved writing it and are inspired.

Sincerely,

Shauna

Blog Post: Late 2014

I have recently discovered and become obsessed with travel novels. The one currently taking space on my night stand is the travel memoir of a single woman off to see the world after years of chasing the American dream. So far it's overshadowed with her promiscuity and mish-mash of one night stands and shallow sexual experiences... not the story I am actually interested in. As I am finishing the book, I feel like I know more about her long lost string of lovers but have forgotten where she actually travelled. However, it was her reference to a double life that really got my attention and I realized as I read further that I have been living a double life too. Within the first few pages I have discovered that I have a fairly significant case of Wanderlust. And what is Wanderlust? I thought you would never ask! Here is the exact Webster's dictionary definition:: A strong desire to wander and explore the world.

Yep, that's me! I have a husband and three kids whom I love dearly. I call a loving community of like-minded believers my church home and have loads of cherished friends and family. I work a couple of part time jobs that I enjoy as well as help with a successful business, and have lots of hobbies and interests that fill up my spare time. But I only have two real passions: God and travel. It's been that way for as long as I remember.

Having a passion for travel isn't nurtured by going to Mexico once a year or living for road trips. Those are enjoyable, but they're vacations. A passion for travel goes much deeper. I used to think everyone felt it, but sometimes I would find myself talking about my dreams of living internationally, or how I could easily be a missionary in Africa, or how I get lost in imagining running a beach bakery on some island. Most often, in response, I would get looks, as if people were thinking, "That's interesting but no thanks, not for me." It didn't appear to be something they ever connected with. So eventually I stopped sharing or talking about it. My passion for travel went from being something that drove me to something that I kept to myself.

This is how the author explains it in this latest book. She describes secretly saving money to travel like it was a silent fever. She says her wanderlust had been in abeyance, like a briefly dormant volcano. She pondered that there was so much of the world she hadn't seen yet. There were lives she hadn't experimented with. What if she was meant to be a dive instructor, a spy? What if she was meant to be a writer in New York? What would it feel like to just wander the world, free of all responsibility, knowing she could stand on her own two feet? She questions it all.

Clearly, she is a single woman, footloose and fancy free. Clearly, I am not. But oh my word, did she just crawl in my head and write down exactly what I think and how I feel? I crave culture and food; ancient architecture; history; experiences; waterfalls and cobblestone streets; the ocean; the desert; new stories from new friends; Spanish and French language; walks on the beach; adventure and excitement. Most of all, I crave change. I need change. My nightstand is piled high with tour company books; itineraries; National Geographic and Caribbean Life magazines; and an iPad bookmarked with wait for it… all things travel and missions and adventure! Travel for me is getting to know the world personally. I had never read words on paper that so eloquently and perfectly described the condition of my head and on an even deeper level, of my heart. For the first time, I didn't feel alone with my thoughts. I realized there were others like me.

It doesn't help that my adult pursuit of the American dream hasn't really satisfied anything in my soul. This is my double life. Essentially I have spent 20 years working really hard with a packed family schedule, running around meeting deadlines at frantic paces, all to earn a small vacation each year. Yes I have food on my table, a vehicle, a home, and healthcare. Compared to 95% of the rest of the world I am considered rich and I am thankful. But overall I would trade it in a heartbeat for a simpler and more meaningful life. Travel, to me, is simpler. Travel is meaningful.

Our short vacations don't satisfy my soul's craving and I doubt they ever will. I'm conservative and pensive, and a minimalist in every way. I loathe stuff. And things. I despise consumerism. I choose experiences instead, any day of the week. My possessions are thin and my closets hold only necessities. I am deeply spiritual. Every day is a culture clash for me and I feel lost. I know where I am, but I'm in the wrong place. I suppose that's where God comes in. I can try to live my life as it is now for Him and not just for myself. I choose to believe that God has placed certain desires and dreams in me, that aren't meant to just stay there forever, stagnant and unfulfilled. I believe that life is a journey, with twists and turns, ups and downs, seasons, valleys, and mountains. God walks with me, teaching me, training me, leading me, even preparing me perhaps. But for what? I still have no idea, but in the meantime I choose to settle. To stay where I'm at, and do all that is required of me. To serve here if that is what God wants. Be salt and light. Ready and waiting to help in any way I can. But underneath I am craving something very different. Change, I pray, is on the horizon.

PROLOGUE

I remember it like it was yesterday. Breakfast was cooking, lunches were being packed, the boys were gathering their belongings for school, and my hubby Clint was having his coffee. The only thing unusual about the day was the background noise. Strangely, the TV was on. And there she was. Heather from Toronto, mother of two sweet boys, being interviewed on Canada AM with her husband about their upcoming year-long trip around the world. She was a travel blogger and her hubby was taking a sabbatical. The kids would be learning on the road, she explained. Their house was already rented out, and they were packing their bags, their kids giddy with excitement. The countdown to departure day had begun. I listened intently. *Who does this!* It was way more of a statement than a question. *We could do this! Couldn't we? We could totally do thi*s. The idea to take our boys and travel around the world was born that morning in the kitchen. I was instantly inspired. Stirred. Motivated. This had to happen for us. I knew right then and there that I wanted it.

It would be foolish to think I just woke up that day looking for something new for us to do. The truth was that we were still settling in from our previous "new thing for us to do." Just 3 years previously, we'd uprooted our comfortable life, packed up our brand new dream home, moved provinces, left all the family and friends we had—essentially our complete support system, bought a business basically on a whim, and left. Settled into our new community, life was awesome, actually. Our business was doing well; our kids were settled into their new home and school; we found a fantastic church family and lots of new friends. We had absolutely nothing to complain about. We had no regrets. But when you think like I do, you're never done dreaming, and never feeling settled. It's a relentless pursuit of what's next. Change-chasing. *There must be more.* I can't honestly say Clint was always like this; he was settled when I met him, but more recently he was always up for a new adventure. The monotonous life of eat, work and barely play was starting to get old again. The occasional travel we dabbled in over the years, whenever we found small amounts of time and money, had whet his appetite for something out of the ordinary. Our conversations about returning home from vacations always went something like this:

Me "So? Are you ready to get home?"

Him "Not really. I'm always anxious to get back and get making money again, but it's not like I'm missing home or anything. Are you?"

Me "Uhh, no. I'm never ready to go home. And it's not just the relief from reality or the rest and relaxation. It's the change of pace. The sun. New scenery. Being on an adventure. Every day looking forward to something new and interesting."

Him "You don't miss people? Your bed? Your own space? Routine?"

Me "No. Never. I dread it."

Him "Yeah I guess I get that, I'm kind of the same. I just start to feel the pinch of how business is doing and I feel like the longer we're gone, the more money we spend and I just start thinking about what's gone wrong and which customer is choked about something. But overall, I could stay here or wherever forever, or at least for longer. I don't have a super strong connection to being in Canada or anything."

Me "I do think we're different from other people in that way. I hear my friends and family, usually ready to get back to reality at the end of a vacation. To the comforts and routine of home. Their space. Friends and family. That's just not me at all. I feel weird about it I guess."

Him "Yeah well, maybe someday we'll venture off and do something crazy and then we'll know for sure."

Clint was stirred, like me. I, however, had felt antsy for a while. Two years before our big move, nine friends and I, all of us moms, had the opportunity of going to Guatemala on a mission trip for ten days. We'd planned for months. We held fundraisers; learned Spanish songs and skits; and packed hockey bags with soccer balls, school uniforms, and shoes. It was exhilarating. My boys were only four years, two and a half years, and nine months old. I left home tired but excited.

I remember vividly our arrival at the airport and rushing to use the woman's washroom, to find the garbage piled high with used toilet paper. Someone explained to us that the sewer system wasn't able to break down toilet paper, so we left our First World ways behind and adapted to wiping and leaving it in the provided garbage bin. We were reminded that water is a commodity and not to be wasted, so not to let it run while we brush our teeth or wash our face. We were given a flat pillow and a sheet for sleeping, with just a thin foamie underneath. There was no air conditioning and the heat was debilitating, so the sheet became more of a barrier between us and the starving mosquitos and less about warmth. I remember the stench of smoke in the air and watched it billow into the skyline day after day. Kim, our trip host, explained that in Guatemala they don't have a specific place to haul their trash, much less environmental laws regarding burning garbage and so he confirmed, the smell was, in fact, burning garbage. The locals literally burned it in their yards or hauled it to a large pit in a jungle valley where it just burned all day long. I was uncomfortable more times than not, but I loved every challenging moment.

We spent hours in an orphanage playing silly games with the kids, and teaching English. We ministered in local churches, sharing our testimonies and performing our goofy skits in terrible Spanish to laughter and applause. We ventured door-to-door in local villages, sharing stories about how God had changed us and teaching our listeners who Jesus was. We brought Bibles and tracts to a local federal men's prison where I slithered to the front to stand before two hundred criminals in my sweat-drenched flip flops, terrified and grasping for my notes that I had forgotten on the breakfast table. I had already realized on the bus ride that I'd left them behind but was still desperately hoping they would appear in my hand. In my panic and distress I hoped God would slip them to me anyway. He did not. I don't hear directly from God much, if ever, but the night before I had a very distinct sense that I was not to bring notes to the prison, and to speak from my heart spontaneously as God led me, not according to the script I had meticulously prepared. I wrote the notes anyway, so it came as no surprise that I forgot them and even less of a surprise that God didn't bail me out. But I'm human and I was in full-panic mode. To this day, I have no idea what I said up there in front of all those eyes. I'm sure it was ok. This was pre-Instagram Story days, even pre-iPhone days. There is no record of what any of us shared, but the prisoners clapped and seemed to appreciate our efforts and we finished by praying with them.

I still don't know why Guatemala was so life changing. I spent a large portion of my time there in tears, just crying and crying. I couldn't stop. There was some friction among the women on the trip which I may have felt obliged to sort out, but overall, I just felt a sense of sadness in Guatemala and couldn't shake it. I remember calling Clint and telling him all about it, imagining aloud that we could return as missionary hosts, living on base as a part of this amazing organization. We could do whatever jobs needed doing. I didn't care, I just didn't want to go home. I wanted a piece of this pie, whatever pie it was. Clint was less than enthusiastic, as any husband left at home would be, keeping the hamster wheel of a household of three kids under age five spinning. Looking back, I realize that I sounded emotional and probably even delusional to him, but I definitely meant it. The last memory I have of Guatemala, besides racing through airports to catch our connecting flight home, was driving out of the city. I was crying again, my head resting on the bus window. We slowed to a stop sign and a sweet strange man noticed me crying. In an attempt to comfort me, he approached my side of the bus and drew a heart in the dust on my window and then walked away. *Do you know him??* I remember someone from my team asking with shock. *No*, I laughed. *I don't even know where we are.* But it felt meaningful and personal. I was speechless and moved to even more tears. I loved my time in Guatemala, but it wrecked me. For months.

Blog Post: Late 2016

It's hard to say when it started. It wasn't long ago that the feeling of change in the air brought us here to Kamloops! Eight years later now, and we are ready for something new again. How did we decide to just sell off, pack up and go travelling for a year? It was in June of 2011 the day the idea sparked, with Canada AM on the tv quietly in the background. The kids shuffled out the door to school. Clint left and I retreated to the computer to do emails and check Facebook. Suddenly my attention was drawn to the story on the tv. Seeing that family about to leave on a one year trip around the world amazed me. I was struck with awe and wonder and of course, complete inspiration. It was exactly what I wanted. So I went completely against my will and did something I never do: I left it with God and prayed… a lot. I told him, "If this is what you want us to do, please tell Clint too." I did not want this to be my big idea again. So, I waited. And waited. And waited. I quietly prepared in the background. I started homeschooling. I researched. I continued to wait.

Two years later, my wonderful husband came home from work one day and, over dinner, casually mentioned that he had spotted an RV beside him at an intersection on the way home.

"Wouldn't it be cool," he said, "to just sell the business and travel with the kids for a year?"

I was so excited and overwhelmed. I was touched, feeling for one of the first times in my life that God really heard my prayers. That moment was far from the end; it was actually only the beginning of the process. It took another six months for Clint to be actually ready to list our business, another few months after that until we found an interested buyer, and then another two and a half years for the deal to close. So yes, five years! That's the short version. I'm leaving out the gory details, the tears, the limbo, the frustration, the giving up of more than one dream to be replaced by new ones and all the sadness that comes with so much uncertainty, just to name a few.

But the time has finally come. We're here now and I'm not quite ready to look back yet. Maybe at some point I'll be able to reflect and see the lessons or purpose if it's there in the whole thing but not yet… In the meantime, I'm on my way to Fiji!

CHAPTER 1

Pre-Trip

The big move to British Columbia followed my Guatemalan adventure by a couple of years. In time I'd recovered from being wrecked. As in, I'd stopped crying. But the longing for change nestled deep in me. I was pacified for a short while. The move was a change at least, which is what I craved, but it was still life in North America: work, eat and barely play. Business kept us tied down. Years when we had good employees allowed us a week off for a road trip, or, best case scenario, a cruise booked between long weekends because God forbid we'd be gone too long. Clint always spent our time away dodging emails and would return to lagging sales and fires to put out. We were rarely gone long enough for him to even begin to rest. Was it really worth it? I nestled my newest little dream in the quiet corners of my heart, sharing it occasionally with a friend or two, but most often with God. He knew. I pulled the boys out of school at their request and learned how to homeschool them. Our first curriculum was Countries and Cultures, how fitting! I scoured the internet for itinerary ideas, flight options, treks, accommodation leads, relocation cruises, and costs. The dreaming had begun! I stumbled upon groups of people who not only travel full time, but tote their kids around the world in much the same way I wanted to. They called it WorldSchooling. A lifestyle - who knew? I soaked up as much information and inspiration as I could and I continued to dream. For almost two long years, I never spoke a word about it to Clint. I discovered couchsurfing, WorkAway, HelpX, Servas

International, house-sitting, and home-swapping. So many options for travel. There were people out there like me, and many of them! I never felt crazy in those online groups. They were my people... my secret life. I asked a billion questions. I watched and I learned. I waited.

And then it happened. One day out of the blue, exactly as my best girlfriend had predicted it would. "He'll just come home one day and blurt it out, you know," she told me. "You watch." And he did. In that same kitchen where it sparked in my heart and mind while watching that TV program two years earlier. He brought it up between bites of dinner.

"I think we should just sell the business and travel with the kids for a while. I was parked beside an RV at the lights coming home and I thought, how cool would it be to just go?"

I smiled.

"What's so funny?" he asked.

"Oh nothing, I just got this idea a long time ago but I've been praying about it and have been waiting for you to hear it from God too."

"Where would an idea like that come from for you?"

I knew the traveling the world part would be a bit much for him but I decided to mention it anyway. "Well, my idea is a little bigger but it's in the same hemisphere. I heard a woman on TV one morning sharing about how she and her family were leaving to travel the world for a year and I fell in love with the idea. I didn't realize anybody even did that with kids."

"Well, I didn't say anything about travelling around the world. I said renting a motorhome and travelling North America," he stated flatly. "We're definitely not doing that."

"Ok, well we'll see how it goes," I replied. "Let's talk about selling the store and see where it goes from there."

Clint's idea of travel wasn't exactly the same as my idea... yet, but we were getting closer. The dream had just moved from being nestled privately in my heart to being discussed. We were expressing ideas out loud. Together. Neither of us had any idea where it would all lead.

The decision and process to actually list and sell our business played out like a slow-moving, overly drawn-out movie you just want to finish and get over with. We listed it within months of our initial conversation and had a fairly quick offer that we accepted right away. Then the waiting game began. The offer was from a lovely Indian couple that we met and instantly liked. They were around our age and were using a program offered by the BC government aimed at pairing international buyers with eligible businesses to secure immigration to Canada. It came with extra paperwork and government involvement. The six to nine month proposed closing time frame was a little out of our comfort zone, but we weren't exactly packed and ready to leave. With a positive attitude, we chalked it up to having extra preparation time, took a significant deposit, and signed off on the deal. However, the deal was far from done. Six to nine months turned into twelve months, which then became eighteen months. Eighteen months bloomed into two years.

We lived in constant limbo, being only a government email away from an approval for our buyers to move forward. It was constant email checking. Talking about it became tiresome.

We're leaving soon.

We're not leaving soon.

Why aren't you gone yet?

You're still here?

We thought we couldn't register the kids for sports, then another delay would come and we would register late and have to pay extra fees. We couldn't plan vacations. We could barely plan company. It was emotional and frustrating and sad and difficult for all of us. We wanted to back out of the deal, but were too far along in the process. It felt as though it would never end. The kids didn't understand what was happening and the constant barrage of repetitive questions from people who couldn't figure out what we were actually waiting for made it frustrating to even go out. I watched the timelines of my meticulously-planned trip itineraries come and go multiple times. The boys became pre-teens and teens and were growing increasingly resistant to the idea at all. They were deeply planted in community sports, church youth groups and friendships. Our dream trip did not align with what they wanted at all. All of the waiting had changed their minds.

And then the email arrived - the buyer had been approved. We cheered but discovered it was too soon to celebrate yet. He still had to get a visa. We were in constant contact with them in India, finalizing details, finishing paperwork, processing the transfer of franchisees. Four months later, still no visa.

I felt crazy.

Full blown I-can't-do-this-anymore-I'm-done crazy.

I cycled through tears, depression, complete and total frustration. I, at least, was free to spend afternoons in bed, unwilling to face the reality of the day. Clint still had to get up and get to work to keep the business running. I just wanted to sleep. *Someone just wake me up when this is all over.* Yet another departure date came and went. By September the school year got underway and the pressure to return by the following summer because of school in the fall, was shortening up every plan I had come up with. I didn't even know where we were going anymore. Tensions were thick with the kids. Carson, my oldest, was officially not playing hockey and had to listen to hear all about it as his friends' seasons went into full swing. The kids' schoolwork was disjointed and basically non-existent, since my mind was disjointed and basically non-existent. The calendar came at us from all angles, reminding them of every upcoming event that they wouldn't be around for. There were endless questions, and no answers, and all I could do was cling to prayer and solitude and try to make sense of why and for what possible purpose God would take us through this. Sometimes, as parents, we keep our struggles private from our kids. We attempt to shelter them from our own questions and concerns.

I didn't.

I let it all out. I apologized that it appeared like their dreams were being shelved for a dream of mine that wasn't even coming to fruition. I felt terrible for everything that they feared missing out on: the senior year of hockey; the friends they feared would forget them; the youth group sleepovers and retreats that might never happen again; ski season; the list went on and on. As adults we have the rationale to understand that these things are replaceable, but to teens these things feel like their whole life. My kids were suffering. We were trying to cling to hope. I made repeat calls to our local government MLA's office, giving our details, praying that she could pull some strings. *Get this guy his visa!* Another month would pass in silence. My last call to her office included tears and a complete breakdown. Finally, the next morning, the email arrived. Our buyer had his visa. His flights were booked. I was almost too tired and frustrated to care.

The next six weeks were chaos. We rented out our house fully-furnished but had to pack up bedding, linens, and family photos which all had to be packed up and stuffed into rubbermaid bins and left in closets throughout the house. We researched and bought backpacks, carry-on bags, travel cubes, wet shoes, windbreakers, travel towels, sunscreen, adapters, chargers, earbuds and ear plugs. Amazon became my daily go-to. We moved into a friend's home for two weeks while we transitioned out of the business and Clint trained the new owner. We had to pack and separate clothes according to season and climate for varying portions of our trip. I cancelled utility bills; forwarded mail; spent hours preparing our business year end; poured over contracts; tried to keep our house clean and organized; closed the pool. We somehow showed up presentable almost every night to going-away dinners and parties during our final two weeks in town. Passports and all ID and credit cards had to be photocopied and put online into file storage. We had to draw up a will, organize long-term travel insurance, perform a final count of business inventory. Two and a half years after we accepted the offer on the business, and almost five years after my dream sparked that morning in my kitchen, we finally passed the last eight years of our livelihood onto someone else. We put the cheque in the bank, blew out the candles on our last "Adios" cake, and on November 11, 2016, we packed our van for the big road trip south and hit the road. Carson was almost 15 and in Grade 9, Braden was 13 and in Grade 8 and Rylan was 11 and in Grade 6. *No looking back!* Except of course, when Clint realized ten minutes down the road that he forgot his sunglasses back in his truck. He will definitely need those! First stop - Wal Mart.

Blog Post: November 2016 (1)

I've covered the when, where and why. So, what are we doing and how are we going to do it? I hate to sound like a broken record, but this plan has changed SO many times, who knows where it will go from here? But I have to start somewhere!

First off, the money. Everyone wants to know, how much will this cost, and where on earth are we going to find that amount to spend? I hate talking about money and I'd love to just say it's personal but honestly, people are interested and many would be shocked to know it isn't necessary to be wealthy in order to explore the world. Budget travel is completely possible. I've been following hundreds of travelling families online for years and am confident it can be done inexpensively. We certainly won't be staying at big-budget all-inclusive resorts, going on high-end tours, or flying first-class. We will travel comfortably, but not extravagantly. Typically a person will travel how they live. If you live lavishly, you'll likely travel that way. If you live conservatively, you will travel on a fairly strict budget. To our friends I would say - if you know us, you know how we live. Enough said.

So here it is, the mysterious amount! Our travel budget is $50,000 CAD.

Yes, we sold our business and have the money. Not everyone has the same opportunity. This was part of our plan and we made it happen in this way. We also had no personal debt to worry about, meaning that there won't be any bills to pay while we travel besides keeping our house and two cars. For other people, this part of the plan could look completely different.

The amount budgeted was supposed to last for a year. Our trip will be much shorter now but that doesn't mean we cut the budget. No way, man. It just means we're throwing in a cruise! That's my treat for having to slash an entire continent from my original plan. Yes, poor me, I know. No one is feeling sorry for me, but anyone who knew how much I wanted to go to Peru would understand how much the slash hurt. For me, this trip was about Peru from the beginning, For two years the whole plan revolved around Peru, but we couldn't make it work. We had a moment of silence on the way to church one morning for Peru when I broke the news to the family that it got scratched. Literal silence. My family all knew how badly I wanted it. And yes Geography Police, I know Peru is not a continent but when it got slashed, so did all of South America. And Central America too. Mexico has snuck back in recently but that's another post.

Back to the money. How will $50,000 CAD stretch over a year? Well, I haven't left my kitchen table yet, so nothing is written in stone, but I am confident in my plan. Here's a snippet:

1. *Saved Travel Points: Two years ago, in preparation, I took out three credit cards with the best free points offers. Every dollar we've spent, business and personal, has gone on the cards. Even just parking - it goes on the card. We have enough points saved to cover approx 50 nights of the most basic hotel rooms that each program covers. Of course, if we stay in nicer rooms, the points won't go as far. I am pleased. Pretty good payback for just our normal spending habits.*

2. *Free Stays: We will be staying in Australia for three months, mostly with Clint's brother's family. They even have a car for us to borrow. We won't stay there the whole time but it will be our home base on the continent and that is a huge budget boost. One week was gifted to us half-price in Fiji, and two weeks were gifted to us in Mexico (which is why it got added back into the itinerary.) When we go to Haiti, we will stay with friends who live there as well.*

3. *House-Sitting and Hospitality: We are registered with every couch surfing, hospitality program, house-sitting, and homestay website out there. These are super popular options in the travel community. We've already secured our first house-sit in Brisbane right after Christmas, close to my in-law's place. It is a free place to stay, with a pool, in exchange for caring for the big house and a few pets. Two words... no brainer. We went through a rigorous application process and are approved Servas International travellers. This will allow us short stays with strangers whenever it suits us. We hosted couch-surfers throughout the last year so we have a good feel for what that will be like.*

4. *Combining Points: We are also registered on every hotel, car rental, travel booking site out there and have points accounts with all of them. For most bookings online, we will be quadruple-point dipping between cash back points, free rooms from hotels.com, hotel chain collector points, and credit card points. Tired yet? Now you know what I've been doing hiding at home for two years. Last week, just from paying the deposit on our cruise and our Australia flights I earned enough points for three free nights in a hotel.*

5.   *Budget Flights: Once you leave Canada, flying gets dirt cheap. I've carefully planned all of our flights one-way and direct, which is a much cheaper way to book. For all five of us, for the entire trip leaving from, then returning to LAX, it will be around five flights costing approximately $12,000 CAD. Total! Only one flight is booked at the moment, and things may change slightly, but not by thousands. And again, I have points collector numbers for every airline we're using and have figured out how to pool points between airlines—strategies that will bring further deals.*

6.   *Surplus Income: We also have our house-rental income which is enough to cover all of our static payments plus create a small pool to cover anything unexpected. We're additionally stockpiling our "Trudeau bucks" coming in every month, which of course our kids will be paying back 10 years from now in taxes but it's free money for now. Dear Children, you can sort it out later, enjoy your trip. Love, Trudeau.*

So that's the how. Here's the what... aka the plan. This is not the original plan, or even the second or third plan. Somewhere closer to the fifth plan, it is a whole new itinerary based on the season, departure time, and predetermined return time based on the school year. The boys will be returning to a brick-and-mortar school when we get back.

Mid-November: Drive to Phoenix to leave our van at my cousins, then rent a car to complete the drive to LAX.

Late November - February: Three months in Australia - via a three-week layover in Fiji.

March: Two weeks in Southern Thailand followed by two weeks in Northern Thailand? / Vietnam? / Cambodia? while Carson meets up with our church youth group there for a short-term mission trip.

Early April: Three to five days in the United Arab Emirates. Cruise from Dubai for sixteen days visiting Oman, Suez Canal in Egypt, Haifa and Nazareth in Israel, Jordan, Athens in Greece, with our final port in Venice, Italy.

Mid-April: Three weeks overland travel from Italy to London, England.

Early May: Fly from London back to Cancun for two weeks in Mexico.

May: Fly from Cancun back to Los Angeles. Drive through the southern United States to Florida, then two weeks in Haiti to see friends.

June - August: Three-month road trip up the east coast of the USA to Canada, then west across Canada, home to BC.

That's a wrap! Five years of waiting and dreaming concluding in a ten month world tour of sorts. Lots of blog posts will be coming. Can't wait to share it all with you! xo

One week. Feels like it's been much longer. Fiji has been good to us so far, but we're already feeling the difference between travel and vacation for sure. We parked ourselves for the first six nights at a local backpacker "resort" within walking distance of the beach. It was a slight risk, committing that long, knowing it wasn't a high-end hotel. Our first impressions were jarring, coming off of the plane after basically pulling an all nighter ('cuz who really sleeps on the plane?!) and being whammed with choking humidity and heat.

After a very annoying wait at the airport, since our shuttle wasn't there as expected, we finally arrived at our hotel. This turned out to be our first experience in a VERY long list of ways 'Fiji Time' isn't just a reference to a slower pace of life. It is THE way of life.

Fijians don't just do things slowly, they barely do some things at all, and some things just never happen. Fiji Time is:

'I'll let you know.'

'I'll call you.'

'It will be there soon.'

'Yes darling, right away,' (meaning never).

Fiji Time is rooms ready without all of the beds even set up, no towels, and 'free' Wi-Fi meaning no Wi-Fi. Fiji Time means that the advertised fitness gym is under renovations, which means that actually, the key is missing and no one cares to find one. Fiji Time includes being told the hotel is 2 km farther and left, when actually it is 20 km farther and right. And, that the turn-off we need to take is two hundred m past the 'steep hill' only to find ourselves going up and over several hills, debating which one would be considered steep. We quickly had to understand and accept Fiji Time, remembering this isn't a vacation. We're not being pampered and doted on in a five-star hotel.. Fiji Time speeds up a little, I assume, for those dishing out big bucks and not chumming it local style.

Other adjustments from our first week: we've sunburned and peeled; tried to sleep through jets taking off and landing over our heads; driven half an hour too far twice; and been through three rental cars. We had just celebrated Clint successfully driving on the left side of the road for ten minutes when BAM he smoked a curb, blew a tire, and limped it banging along until we could park safely in front of a potato farmer's stand. We had no cell phone, and the car had a broken jack and wrong-sized spare tire.

Thank God for Fiji Man #1 who called the rental company, for Fiji Man #2 and #3 who had actual jacks that work, and for what might be the only rental car company in all of Fiji that doesn't run on Fiji Time. They were there in 10 minutes, as promised, with a new car for us. Picture Fiji Man #3's surprise as our three boys, who had been banished in silence to the back seat for half an hour while we sorted everything, out, finally piled out from behind tinted windows to get into the new car. He had no idea they were in the back. I thought the guy was going to laugh his life away! The third car was a swap as the second one had been previously booked. So here we are with a third car in four days. Good times.

Let me tell you, I honestly wouldn't trade any of it. We spent yesterday afternoon touring Denarau Island which is where we finally found the white people on vacation. I knew they were here somewhere. This is a small area outside of Nadi where there are eight five-star hotels, a water park and a fantastic golf course. It left my kids' mouths agape, wondering why we aren't staying there. At first I regretted bringing them. I know full-well that was more their style. And I can't lie, we would have had an amazing and relaxing, five-star time if we did. But the whole purpose of this trip is to experience the world, not just take a holiday. We made the decision a while back that we would sacrifice a lot of luxury in order to gain that experience, even if it meant a stretch, or in some cases a serious jog, out of our comfort zone. We all agreed that we would never have the Fiji experience treating it like a vacation. Most vacationers who come never even leave the island. No thanks. We've driven all over the place; shuffled our way through the locals in downtown Nadi; raced through the veggie market at closing, bargaining and buying; attended a local church service; lathered ourselves in mud and soaked in hot pools; eaten hard boiled eggs and canned pork and beans for breakfast; and learned that black bananas in Fiji are not over-ripe, they are the absolute best, and that you haven't lived until you've tried roadside pineapple! At one point we all did agree that we're here for the experience. At this point however, we're just agreeing to disagree that we're all on the same page about that. I guess appreciation will come later.

Even though the first hotel came with disappointments and frustrations, we found ourselves feeling VERY thankful for some luxuries. The beds were extremely comfy. We were surprised that there was air conditioning because we thought our room only came with a fan. There was plenty of hot and cold water, good showers and good toilets. I like a good toilet. The drinking water has been great, and the food has been delicious. Who could complain about there being sunshine all day every day? And the people? Overall, they are lovely. Costs have been much higher than we had hoped. Even doing things locally and off the beaten path, we've still been paying way more than we anticipated. We've been sharing meals, trying to stuff ourselves on free breakfast, and are barely having any treats. A can of Coke anywhere is $3 CAD, and a small block of cheese is $6 CAD. We haven't had a meal yet under $45 CAD. Not highway robbery, but just much higher than we had expected.

Today we changed things up, drove along the coast, and checked into The BeachHouse, a lovely backpacker resort right on the beach. Everyone ventured off right away, exploring the sand; wading out into the low tide; kayaking; sucking up good free Wi-Fi; playing pool and ping pong; and braving sleeping in the room with a gecko on the roof. Life is good! We have lots more to see and do this week. Shout out to my hubby! Man, Clint is adventurous. Things that I think will stretch him, he just soaks up the experience and finds some way to love it. His enthusiasm is contagious, I have to say. He has repeatedly said he loves island life and jokes about staying longer. I KNEW it! I knew once he got his butt here he would fall in love. He's the perfect package of positive energy and adventure as a father for our three boys. I'm doing awesome, too. I am sleeping the best I ever have. My tummy feels good. Stress is at an all-time zero (minus experiencing the curb slam.) In the meantime, I can't wait for my two $25 CAD massages this week (a birthday present—thanks Mom and Dad!) I saved my birthday money just for this and it's all mine! Nighty-night friends, from Fiji! xoxo

CHAPTER 2

Fiji

F iji was hot. Bloody hot, and humid. We arrived in Nadi (pronounced Nandi by the locals) at 6:00 am local time, Monday November 20th, on a fairly non-eventful fourteen-hour overnight flight from LA. I say non-eventful loosely as I personally was a basket case. Somewhere between LA and Fiji I acquired a fear of flying and had trouble controlling it. While my seat mates enjoyed the Indian flight food, watched movies, and slept soundly, I was grasping for the paper bag to breathe. *Just breathe. Just breathe. Just breathe.* I could barely eat. Every bump and jump and rumble left me breathless and anxious, my heart pounding. I must have pulled back the window curtain ten times, hoping for a sunset or any sign of light, but it was always just black. I couldn't sleep, nor could I focus. I resigned myself to huffing peppermint oil and repeating Psalm 23 in between constant clock checks.

Yay though I walk through the valley of the shadow of death I will fear no evil… *ten more hours…*

Thy rod and Thy staff, they comfort me… *nine more hours…*

I was ridiculously out of control and it was embarrassing. Unbeknownst to me, these fears, and new ones too, would remain with me throughout our travel. I desperately wanted to travel and thought I'd be awesome at it, but then my body betrayed me. What a head-game! *Was travel anxiety going to be my new normal?*

Before flying, the first leg of our trip driving from Kamloops to LA, via Washington, Idaho, Arizona and California, took almost two weeks. We stopped in Utah to surf sand dunes, tour the Best Friends Animal Sanctuary, explore Zion National Park, and wander the old west town of Kanab. It was tiring but exactly what we needed after the last 6 weeks of preparing. I relaxed almost immediately and quickly adjusted to having Clint around 24/7. Having the kids around already felt normal because of our time homeschooling. My cousin in Phoenix graciously agreed to store the van for six months, so we parked it there and rented a car to LAX, which was much cheaper than any six-month car storage options anywhere near the airport.

The first part of our nine-month itinerary came together in a frenzied six weeks of chaos. After more than two years of delay, all semblance of a plan had been lost, and we had to throw ideas together quickly. I found a great-priced one-way flight from LA to Brisbane, Australia where we had previously planned to spend Christmas with Clint's family. One of the most important things I'd learned during my years of travel research was to look for stopover flights. In my search for flights to Australia, the one that jumped out at me the most was a flight with a three-hour layover in Fiji. From my research I knew that I could divide it into two separate one-way flights. For the same price, we could stretch our three-hour layover into three weeks. And why not? We had nothing but time and almost no new plan yet. And with that, part one was planned out, and it felt wonderful that our trip was coming together with a great start!

No one was waiting for us at the airport in Nadi, even though I had arranged for transportation. But that's Fiji, and the first lesson from our trip. Things do not go as planned outside of North America and rarely does anyone care as much as you do. But it was nothing a phone call and another hour of waiting couldn't fix, and our ride eventually showed up. Lesson two: outside North America and Australia we will likely never wear seat belts. Clint and the driver usually occupy the front seats while the other four of us pile into the back of vehicles. And it doesn't matter how many suitcases you have, they will always fit. This was how our first ride in Fiji went, and we just understood it would be the same from that point on.

As soon as we were loaded, the driver gunned it out of the airport parking lot on the 'wrong' side of the road. We were on our way! Instantly, the temperature was sweltering and the humidity was thick. We peeled off layers of clothing as we drove, and the car was overtaken with the stench of ice-cold cigarette air blasting out of the vents. Something else we figured out very quickly is that people smoke in the rest of the world… a lot. We were just thankful for air conditioning, even if it arrived super smelly. Fiji is a newer country, settled early on by black natives and blended almost equally with Indians who arrived later on. It's a mish-mash of tribal dancing; man-skirts; vibrant flowers; beautiful coconut-scented women; kava ceremonies; curry; and golden delicious to-die-for pineapples. It's India meets Hawaii. We were almost instantly overwhelmed. It was third-world but beautiful and busy, tropical and mesmerizing. I was in heaven and Clint was enthusiastic, but the kids were cautious. We parked ourselves at a lower budget but comfortable enough hotel with a lovely pool (which unfortunately was green for most of our stay.) It included a free breakfast of pork and beans, eggs and toast. Lesson three: pork and beans is normal breakfast fare for most of the rest of the world. This is something Canadians (as a rule) don't do. Our room was missing a bed, but we dozed off by 9:00 am anyway, sucking up every last ounce of cool air from the fan above. Braden and Rylan piled on top of each other on the single bed deep in jet lag slumber, the rest of us sweltered in sweaty comotosis. By early afternoon, we awoke violently to what sounded like a train barreling through our hotel wall. I stumbled, sweaty and delusional, to the window to see the tail end of a jumbo jet 747 landing in our backyard. Our room backed onto a full-scale international airport. *Lovely.* Thank God, Clint later sorted out that we did in fact have air conditioning, tracked down the proper remote for it, and by the afternoon, though we were groggy and disoriented, we were in business, cooling down and re-organizing the room in preparation for the missing bed we were still waiting for.

"What time is it?" Clint asked, in a fog.

It was 1:00 pm. We were starving but had no idea where to eat or what to do. The restaurant at our hotel only served dinner and not until 6:00 pm. We barely knew where we were but someone let us know that there was a beachfront hotel close by that would let us use their beach as long as we ordered food and drinks. We trekked single-file with our backpacks and water bottles along the narrow busy highway. Along the way we came upon a local Indian man with a car trunk full of trinkets and jewelry. He was carving a pineapple and called us over.

"Where you guys from?" he asked.

"Canada," Clint and I replied together.

"Ahh, hockey!" he said excitedly. We laughed and were a little surprised that he knew our national claim to fame so confidently.

"Do you watch hockey?" Clint asked.

"Yeah, I love hockey. I watch it all the time. I love the Oilers, who do you cheer for?"

The boys looked at us with amazement in their eyes. What is the chance of that? We didn't expect to be able to talk hockey for a long time, but especially not in Fiji.

"We're Oilers fans too! We live in BC, where most people cheer for the Canucks, but we're from a different part of Canada originally, so we grew up cheering for Edmonton."

We all laughed and he showed us how to carve pineapple. He offered to carve a fresh one for us that we could all share. We weren't really in the market for a $5 CAD pineapple, but we agreed, chalking it up to our first neat experience in Fiji. He grabbed a ripe pineapple from a box out of his trunk, what looked like a small machete, and hacked and chopped and peeled the long poky peelings away. He handed each of us a chunk and we all savoured the most delicious, sweet and juicy pineapple we had ever eaten in our lives.

Throughout the week that we were there, the staff of the hotel were setting up for Christmas, as best as they could in a third-world tropical country. One morning after breakfast, they put up a sparse, cringy-looking Christmas tree in the middle of the lobby, hung some old christmas balls on each of its branches, and invited us to join them for a kava drinking ceremony later that night. *Sure*, we thought. *That sounds interesting.* Braden and Rylan weren't interested, so after dinner the other three of us joined in a circle of people sitting on the floor of the main gathering room. They mixed kava root powder with warm water into a drink and we passed bowls around. As it came to each of us, we took a sip from our bowl and were instructed to clap once and yell "Bula!" It didn't have much of a taste. My main concern was wondering when the bowls we were all sharing were last washed! The hosts told funny stories, sang Fijian songs and explained to us that this was a very traditional thing to do. It relaxes people and helps them resolve conflicts with each other, which makes perfect sense when you discover that the kava root has anesthetic and sedative properties. It's basically used in Fiji to get mildly drunk or at least very relaxed. We took our sip and were satisfied with just that.

My gang, in the end, didn't have great impressions of Wailoaloa Beach Resort. It was not, in fact, beachfront, as had been advertised. I booked it specifically so Carson could use the gym, which never opened and no one could tell us why. There was no Wi-Fi. The 'full kitchen' turned out to be two plates, two knives, and an electric pan that we used to boil eggs. Planes landed loudly several times each day. I was grateful for air conditioning and comfy beds and decided to pick my battles knowing that there were likely to be worse hotels in our near future. And it was from here that we discovered a little gem just down the road. We stumbled upon *Grace Road Kitchen* while searching for somewhere budget friendly to eat. Nothing is budget friendly in Fiji.

A lovely Korean woman stood outside the restaurant, waved us over and introduced herself. She seemed overly friendly but now I think she was trying to rescue the poor white family from being conned into paying $5 CAD for a roadside pineapple. While perusing the menu it seemed the place was Christian-run. I came right out and asked her if it was.

"Yes!" she said.

"So are we!" I blurted back. We found an instant Christian connection and Korean food heaven. She explained how the restaurant was run by a Korean organization that came to Fiji to grow rice sustainably, create jobs, and teach the locals how to cook Korean food, all while telling them about God. This was their third restaurant on the island. The food was amazing and relatively inexpensive. We ate stir fried noodles, spicy rice, and cassava chips three times that week. It was divine!

I booked four different places to stay in three different areas of Fiji so we could explore various locations on the island. Wailoaloa Beach Resort is seared into our memory as our first stop on our world tour, and it also included our first cockroach sighting. It was also the place Clint could never pronounce. He confused taxi drivers with something sounding like 'Wallawalla' while we died laughing in the back seat. To be precise, it is pronounced "WhyLowaLowa." While staying there we had our very first beach visit, watching the kids run on the sand and swim in unbelievably warm water. While in Nadi we explored the local market for fresh veggies and fruit and eggs to cook in our terribly ill-equipped kitchen. We bought our first souvenirs—the boys all bought Fijian dress shirts which would come in handy for all of the church services we participated in for the remainder of the trip.

We met memorable people like Krish, the taxi driver from our first day who became a friend and go-to for all things Fiji that we couldn't figure out on our own. He even gave Clint a quick driving lesson before we rented our first car. Fiji was our first experience driving on the left side of the road. It was sad to eventually have to say good-bye to Krish, the first friend of our travels.

Going to church around the world was one of the things I had been most excited about. While there were many Christian services available in the Nadi area, finding one in English proved difficult. After asking around, we made our way to a Sunday service in a local hotel conference room and were warmly welcomed. The room was filled with a comfortable mix of ethnicities and we didn't stand out too drastically as we made our way to seats somewhere in the middle. There wasn't a fancy smoke and light show, a band, or even any instruments. We sang from hymnals acapella which was definitely a first for all of us. I couldn't help but close my eyes and take in the booming voices of three large black men singing out to God from the front of the room. It was so simple, so reverent, and so comforting. We took communion, listened to a great message and testimony, and prayed. It was just like church as we know it, except it was Fiji. It was magical but we also felt right at home. After the service, we chatted with some locals and helped ourselves to soup and juice. It was a great first church experience and I was so thankful we made it happen.

Our second stay was at The BeachHouse, a family-friendly hostel located halfway between Nadi and Suva on the Southeast coast of the island, a two-hour drive from where we had been in Nadi. Meals were included in the price as well as access to a beautiful beach, water activities, a great social area, and lots of reasonably priced tours. On the downside, there was no air conditioning, and no hot water in the showers, which were public. We experienced our first bunk beds of the trip and the hostel had misplaced our reservation; par for the course in Fiji, we were learning.

While checking in, the gentleman searching for our reservation on his computer for much longer than it should have taken him to find it. I sighed inwardly knowing they were not prepared for our arrival.

"We don't have you reserved here ma'am," he said with a nonchalant air.

I pulled up the reservation on my phone and showed him the details.

He shrugged. "Well, we'll put you in separate bure's tonight and then tomorrow you can move to the bunkhouses in the back."

Sigh. No explanation. No apology. No compensation. Fiji Time.

A Fijian bure is a wood and straw hut, something similar to a cabin. In its original sense, a bure is a structure built of anything that comes in handy, the components are either stacked together, tied together by a rope, or a combination. I had already figured this out in Canada, while researching accommodations and planning our stay.

We shuffled out to our separate bures, where we had to unpack and then repack in the morning to move again. For one glorious night, we had a comfortable queen bed, air conditioning, and a gorgeous outdoor rock waterfall shower. The next four nights were bunk beds, stale sweaty air, and cold showers but the food was always amazing and served in large portions. We stayed for five nights and met great people. We had entertaining and informative conversations throughout the week and compared travel notes with a young couple and a single young woman, Emily, from England. We received a ton of attention for doing what we were doing. People loved our story and always wanted to know how we made it happen. The kids were endlessly reminded how lucky they were, how awesome an experience this would be in their life, and that they would be grateful for it in the future.

"I know, yeah," they would say every time, nodding hesitantly, clearly not quite feeling that gratitude yet.

We snorkelled and ocean-kayaked for the first time at The BeachHouse, and finally learned how to relax. Clint read his first book of the trip, *How Champions Think*, swaying in one of the many hammocks in the palm trees. I have a photo of him reading it while drinking his morning coffee in the glorious sun. The cute grin on his face makes me think he was feeling like quite the champion. We hiked The Jungle Trek with Juta which was a good thing because, as we heard later from many others, *you haven't been to Fiji until you've done the Jungle Trek with Juta*. We gathered at a local bus shelter as Juta sent a random local village child to fetch his running shoes.

While waiting, he took the time to give us an amazing animated history of Fiji and how it was saved from cannibalism by Christian missionaries in the 1830's.

"By the Grace of God!" he exclaimed while wrapping his story up, "My ancestors of this particular village welcomed these Christian teachers and preachers and because of that God has blessed us with good fortune ever since!...by the Grace of God!" You couldn't wipe the joy off of his face if you tried. Juta's shoes eventually arrived and we hit the trail for the waterfalls.

It was gruelling. My anxiety reared its ugly head yet again that day. The trek was only about two hours long but it felt endless. I was exhausted, thirsty, and pouring sweat. But we were only halfway done. We still had to backtrack the whole way to get out! I went into full-blown panic mode and Clint swept into make-it-better mode. He calmed me down enough to finish the hike, and afterward we enjoyed a beautiful and refreshing waterfall swim. Many times through the trip I would appreciate the blessing of my husband's stable, easygoing nature, while feeling frustrated at my new inability to adjust when the going gets tough.

Along the way Juta did such a wonderful job of pointing out local plants and fauna. He told us which plants were used as medicine, how bamboo was used for building, and how the red clay was formed into bowls and pots. *By the Grace of God*, he continually reminded us. When we finally glimpsed the waterfall it was a refreshing sight for sore eyes. And for feet and calves. It was like a tropical waterfall scene out of a movie, one of many such scenes we encountered as time went by. The boys swam out and wasted no time climbing the tall jagged rock backdrop of the booming falls. They barely acknowledged us when we called out that they'd gone high enough. When Juta finally yelled though, they knew he was serious and quickly climbed down.

Juta leaned back on the rock base in the shallow pool and stretched out his legs with his arms behind his head, smiling from ear to ear and offered to take photos. Back at the bus stop he had mentioned that he'd given this exact tour to the falls every day for the last ten years. Every day! He considered it his mission field. Every morning he sauntered into The BeachHouse and rounded up any curious tourists that he could find. He charged $10 which he used to pay the village and local family that fed us a reward of pumpkin curry wraps and fresh coconut water on our way out. He performed this daily ritual with joy and exuberance. *By the Grace of God*, I thought. *By the Grace of God.*

One adventure for the boys was discovering a large gecko on the wall of their bure the night we arrived. We repeatedly told them to go to sleep anyway, trying to assure them it would not hurt them. Hearing all the fuss, a local Fijian boy came to the rescue of my poor Canadian gingers. He seized the poor gecko by the tail and sent it packing. He thought it was hilarious, and must have been rolling his eyes in his head.

We left the BeachHouse rested but sunburnt. Clint and Rylan suffered from heat stroke and were badly dehydrated. Rylan had spent the better part of the previous day in our sweltering room, vomiting and laying in bed with a fever. Clint had ventured out to snorkel with our new friend Emily under overcast skies, finding out the hard way that the sun still makes its way through those fluffy clouds. He was *purple* and in severe pain. I lathered him up with peppermint oil and tylenol and he slept as much as he could in his discomfort. His skin peeled off like a blanket about a week later. It was awful.

The drive to our next place, Fiji Palms, took just over an hour, and of course our rooms were not ready. We dragged our sorry, exhausted, sunburnt bodies to the resort pool next door, dropped into lawn chairs and attempted to stay cool. I ordered pizza and posted a 'keeping it real—life on the road,' post on Facebook while we waited patiently for our rooms. Fiji Palms turned out to be an oasis in the desert, and was situated on a beautiful beach with large lapping waves that the boys adored. We checked in, cranked the air conditioning, and got our first load of laundry going. Clint crashed for two days. We bought groceries and were able to cook, had hot showers in our own bathrooms, and stretched out on our own beds. This stay was a timeshare gift from my parents; we only paid half price for it. It came at the exact moment we needed a reprieve from backpack living. We graciously accepted the gift and appreciated every moment of our stay. Aside from an interesting day trip adventure to Suva that had us temporarily but badly lost, the week spent at Fiji Palms was generally relaxing and non-eventful. We slept late, Clint golfed, and we spent hours at the beach. It was perfect. Our fourth and final stay in Fiji was an airport hotel with a pool and waterslide that I knew the kids would appreciate.

It was located right outside the airport gates, convenient for our early morning flight to Brisbane.

Fiji changed us. It was our first foray into the third world as a family. It was our first adventure with crazy driving, bartering in open air markets, currency and climate adjustments, and our first enjoyment of white sand beaches. But it was a stretch. It was expensive, pushing us over budget almost immediately. The heat and humidity were extremely hard to adjust to, almost unbearable at times. And by the time we left we were already missing cheap treats and familiar food. I was thankful for all of it, the good, the bad, and the ugly—but I expected to feel happier. After years of pre-trip limbo I had grown emotionally weary of the roller coaster ride of frustrated expectations. I was just plain tired and down and having trouble shaking it. I noticed an internal wrestling in moments when I should have felt joy but didn't. I realized that I was finally living out the things that I had dreamt about for so long, but was feeling disappointment. This was frustrating and confusing for me, and my family was sensing my inner tension. I loaded 5 years of pressure on this trip to make everything better, to pick me up. We were through the first leg, but really still at the beginning, and I was now on high alert emotionally. *Things probably won't go as planned*, I tried to remind myself and accept. Fiji was done, and it was time to move on. We were ready for Australia and she was ready for us!

> **Travel Tip - Splurge on an island stay or at least an island day pass. The Fijian Islands are where the magic really is and I am still so disappointed that we missed out on exploring them. And don't be afraid to rent a car. Research the company well, make sure it has good reviews and have fun!**

Blog Post: December 2016

Life in Aussie-land is not much different from life up-over. After all, they just talk funny and drive on the wrong side of the road. And the bugs are on steroids! Forget the accent, the English that Australians speak is a whole new language! They speak very literally. Exit is 'way out'; yield is 'give way;' construction pylons are 'witches hats;' and everything gets shortened. Mosquitos to 'mozzies;' swimming costumes (bathing suits) to 'cozies;' barbecues to 'barbies;' and sunglasses to 'sunnies.' You get the pickcha? We are slowly but surely "pardon me-ing" our way around and figuring everything out. I reckon it won't take long!

Clint, thank the good Lord, got over his curb-jumping days in Fiji and we are sailing into smooth waters while driving here. I must say, he seems to know his way around better here than he does back home. Usually I'm the chief navigator, but not so much now, I am twisted around. North is south as east is west. I'm just along for the ride and we're both fine with the change in dynamics!

Clint is enjoying himself exactly as I knew he would, with a beard to prove it! He has already thrown the whole "one year work permit" idea at me. Sounds like a bright idea but we all know he couldn't last that long without Canadian treats like Lays chips, Spitz pumpkin seeds, and NHL hockey—not to worry folks, we'll be comin' home. Getting him back to work might be a different story! He's certainly getting his golf fix.

The kids are settling in amazingly well to our new transient life. We don't give our kids enough credit! No complaining, nothing emotional, zero acting out... they're just having a great time! The timing of being here with family and cousins couldn't have come together better, thank you God. What a blessing to be with Clint's family for Christmas and making all these memories together that will last a lifetime! Carson received a membership to a gym here for his birthday, so we've been running him there and back every other day.

I am pleased to say that I discovered that we have enough points for us to stay in hotels for the entire road trip home! I was so excited the night I figured that out that I almost woke Clint up just to tell him. What a blessing!

But, being the realist that I am, I must clarify that this trip isn't always awesome. We've had to manage some sick days, heat stroke, brutal sun burns, sweltering humidity, some very uncomfortable sleeping accommodations, major budget cuts, and more discussions about what we 'can't afford' than I care to recall. That has quite honestly been the hardest part for me. It is extremely difficult to be a budget traveller in a tourist world. Luxuries that we can't afford are constantly in our face. Kids on vacation want to do everything, buy everything, and see everything. But this is a 10-month trip and it's SO hard and exhausting to constantly say no. Clint and I have gone back to the drawing board several times, hoping to rearrange things, but to no avail. The cruise (which is very meaningful to me) is a huge chunk of the budget and almost got cut. But after spending a week pouring over flights and tours and hotels in Israel trying to piece it together another way, I was left stressed and overwhelmed. So the cruise is back on and I just hope to sweet heaven that we don't regret it. No pressure on me at all!

The good news is, I recently discovered that I can merge points from my two points collector accounts. I only had a small amount of points remaining, but, long story short, the one with more points is worth three times more when I transfer it to the other account. This was amazing news and introduced more possibilities.

As for me, I am doing well overall. I've been learning a thing or two about myself. I've had to wade the waters of disappointment more than I'd like to admit. I envisioned things going differently and perhaps had some unrealistic expectations. It's been nothing that some tears or a good vent to Clint, some prayer time, and a Christmas Eve service at Hillsong Church couldn't fix. But it's been humbling to "live my dream" and figure out nothing is ever perfect. And good grief woman (that's me), it's only been 6 weeks. I need to get out of my head sometimes!

So here we are, with just over two months left here in Australia. We are in the middle of a sweet house and pet sitting gig, with five days to go. The house is huge and has a massive pool and yard. It is very modern and there is tonnes for the kids to do here. What an absolute treat to be here, except for some minor blips like almost backing over a wild turkey in the garage, and having to Google "can dogs eat palm branches?" Welcome to Australia, I guess! When we finish here we will return to my in-laws' place for a week or two, where we are being treated with true Aussie hospitality and feel completely comfortable and at home. But, they need their life back, and we're looking forward to heading up the east coast for a month or so and then back down again before flying to Thailand by the middle of March.

Christmas in the tropics is probably a post in itself but for now we'll just say it has been a different kind of fantastic! We thoroughly enjoyed Christmas Carols by Starlight one night. It was actual carols about Jesus being born, and lots of them, not just Santa songs like in North America! I found shortbread cookies at the local grocery store and was determined to keep Christmas alive with a difficult-t0-find gingerbread house that I finally hunted down on a bottom shelf at Target. We made sugar cookies and homemade cards with the cousins, and watched the most epic Christmas fireworks set to Christmas carols in Southbank Brisbane. There was no turkey dinner for us this year, but we were treated to ham with a potato bake, cold prawns, and salads, finished off with a dessert of pavlova, English trifle, and steamed pudding! It was a true Aussie Christmas, right smack in the middle of summer.

There is so much still to see and do, but in the meantime, enjoy some photos of our adventures and thanks for coming along for the ride!

CHAPTER 3

Australia

Part One

They were waiting for us at the airport, all cute and shy, smiling and waving excitedly. Clint's brother Sheldon, his wife Jennine, and their two kids Jude and Ellie had moved to Australia two years earlier. It had been a bit longer than that since we had seen them, and of course, that was the main reason Australia was on the itinerary. The rough plan was to spend three months in Australia: six weeks with the in-laws, a month-long road trip north, a second family visit, and then a final road trip south along the east coast to depart Melbourne by March. We needed to meet up with our church youth group in Thailand on March 6th. Carson would be joining the team for two weeks for some humanitarian work while the rest of us explored. Aside from the cruise coming up in April, we only had a solid plan for Australia, so beyond that, the world would be our oyster!

Sheldon and Jennine had saved an old car of theirs for us to use while we were exploring Australia, which was a huge blessing and budget saver. *The Red Rocket*, as she became known, was a 1995 Toyota Corolla. We squeezed like sardines into that tiny car, which the kids complained endlessly about, and there was no cruise control, but the trunk somehow fit all of our crap and the air conditioning blew cold. She was rock solid for 3000 kms up and down the east coast and good on gas. The money we saved having her rented us a nicer hotel here and there and probably an excursion or two that we couldn't afford otherwise. We were thankful.

Sheldon and Jennine lived with her parents, Jan and Rob, in her childhood home. We were shown to our rooms after we'd been greeted by a huge and hairy huntsman spider climbing on my chair, whom they swear they had never seen there before! The boys shared a king size and single mattress in an upstairs loft. Clint and I had the caravan (holiday trailer) in the backyard. Other than using the house bathroom, we were self-sufficient. In anticipation of our visit, Sheldon had worked feverishly for weeks pouring a concrete pad and building a roof over a patio area off of the back of the house. They had purchased a ping pong table and set up a lovely outdoor seating area around it. We all spent hours playing ping pong over the Christmas break. Aussie hospitality is world famous and they made us feel so welcome in their home and kitchen. We settled in quickly and adjusted to new ways of doing things while trying to keep our kids and their belongings under control and tidy. We (being I) did our best to keep the kitchen in order and bathroom clean. We bought groceries, shared meal preparation, and got lost and found on our way home many times.

Clint had great aspirations to golf, but Christmas in Australia brings sweltering heat and humidity so, alas, he didn't make it out as much as he wanted to. I enjoyed the comforts of having a home and being able to cook. The kids spent hours working on school work and swimming in the backyard pool in the afternoons, Clint puttered around the yard, mowed the lawn, and helped Rob with anything that came up. Laundry always needed to be hung or taken down from the clothesline, dishes needed washing, toilets needed cleaning, and floors needed sweeping. We revelled in the comfort of having a home away from home while enjoying the newness of things and quirkiness of Australia.

The rest of Clint's family arrived from Canada a week before Christmas for a three-week stay. Those weeks were filled with shopping; bushwalking (hiking); beach breaks; a day trip to Dreamworld (Aussie Disneyland) which was a highlight for the kids; another day trip to Brisbane City; a spectacular Christmas fireworks show one evening; and a Christmas Eve service at Hillsong Church—my highlight by far! If you're a North

American Christian and haven't heard of Hillsong, you haven't left your house. I've stalked Hillsong online for years. I love their music, their conferences, their podcasts, and their books. I even squeezed in their documentary one night before we left Canada in the anticipation of stepping foot into at least one of their campus churches while in Australia. To say I checked a bucket list item when I walked into Hillsong Brisbane would be an understatement. It was *glorious*. The music was emotional and perfect; the Christmas message was touching and personal; the people were lovely; and the Spirit was alive and real. I was so overwhelmed with thanksgiving and gratitude, I didn't even try to hold the tears back as I savoured the sights and sounds and basked in the glory of the moment. I let the frustrations that had been slowly building roll off my back, and shooed my discontentment away for an evening.

As wonderful as Australia had been treating us so far, I had been getting anxious again, feeling bothered by things that were out of my control and nervous about what lay ahead. We had minimal itinerary planned for after the Christmas season, and I hadn't spent five minutes researching our cruise through the Middle East that was quickly approaching. Our close living quarters, minimal alone time, and the addition of Clint's family was wearing down my comfort zone, which was already stretched from living in someone else's home for such a long stretch. Clint's mom was sick and dealing with gruelling prolonged jet lag that left her irritable and frustrated. The house was thick with the tension of trying to keep five teenagers entertained and everyone fed, organized and entertained.

The arrival of our house-sitting dates came just in time. We had signed up to a house-sitting website before we left with the hopes of securing some long-term free accommodation along the way, but so far were only able to secure this one. It was a huge, lovely, newer bungalow with an enormous pool and two dogs to take care of, and was only 5 kms away from Clint's family, so it was a match made in heaven! We moved in on Boxing Day and stayed for a week.

Reflecting back, there isn't much I missed about home while we were abroad. I hate winter with a passion and have no use for snow. I do not need all four seasons. But trying to celebrate Christmas in over forty degree weather with 90% humidity didn't fit for this Canadian. For me, Christmas is white and requires hot chocolate, carols, gingerbread houses, and baking. I longed for cider and sledding and skiing and skating—and oh, the fireplace. Suffice to say, we surrendered to a summer Christmas. I did my best to make sure there were traditional Christmas cookies, though it meant baking in the evening while temperatures were slightly cooler. I bought crafts and played carols and attempted to bring our version of the spirit of Christmas to Australia while still embracing her uniqueness.

Clint's family flew home the first week of January, and we returned to my in-laws' house to spend a few days cleaning and purging and basically regrouping. We also had our second major mishap of the trip (the first being the curb jump in Fiji.) We went to a local trampoline park that the kids would not stop asking to visit. When you find something to do in Australia with good air conditioning, you just go. We paid for them all to go play while I watched and took videos for social media. Clint had decided to try the parkour course and was swinging with glee from the monkey bars and rings, and racing through the obstacles. I recorded a video, and the minute I posted it to social media with the title *Hero Young at Heart Husband—American Ninja Warrior,* one of the boys came running.

"Dad's shoulder is out and he can't put it back in!"

"What do you mean he can't put it back in, what the heck?" I replied.

I went running, hoping he was very wrong, but I found Clint white as a ghost with his arm hanging by the skin and his shoulder socket gaping open. An employee tried desperately to help, but Clint was hopped up on adrenaline and insisted on trying to put it back in himself instead of calling an ambulance. After a few minutes that felt like eternity, he swung it the right way and managed to plop it back in. He just sat there and closed his eyes and breathed huge sighs of relief. Thank God for adrenaline. This was the fifth or sixth time he had dislocated it in his life and we knew he was in for a gruelling, painful healing process. The park employees wrapped him in a sling, hopped him up on Tylenol, and our day at the trampoline park ended almost as soon as it started. Somehow, Clint still managed to drive us home from the right side of the car with the shifter on the left and a freshly re-located left shoulder… in a sling! Good times!

Australia Part Two

Sheldon and Jennine were due back to work soon and their kids would be returning to school, so it was high time we came up with a plan. Rob and Jan had been gracious hosts and nothing but lovely and hospitable but everyone clearly needed a break. And we still hadn't seen a koala bear!

"We need to go find something to do or somewhere to go." I said to Clint, feeling slightly stressed.

I was starting to feel the possibility that we were overstaying our welcome. Not because of anything that had been said or implied, but in all honesty, we arrived without a plan or a departure date and I had no actual idea if they really knew that we had planned on being there for as long as we did. My woman's intuition was picking up that everyone needed a breather.

"Why would we pack up and go anywhere? It will cost a fortune to stay anywhere around here," Clint was not into the idea at all. He preferred free accommodation.

"Because I'm feeling uncomfortable, that's why. We didn't even confirm with Rob or Jan how long we would be here; Sheldon, Jennine and the kids are getting back to their routines. Christmas is over, it just feels like we need to let them have their space back for a bit."

I knew I was in for somewhat of a battle. They don't call it women's intuition for nothing and I knew full-well that Clint felt like I was overreacting.

"No," I said. "I'm not staying here until we leave on our road trip. That's another two weeks down the road! I'll find somewhere reasonable for us to go. I'm sorry but we're leaving for a bit."

Clint disagreed but he knew that I wasn't going to change my mind and after twenty years together we both knew that if I was miserable, he would be miserable. I found an inexpensive apartment in downtown Brisbane on hotels.com. It had a full kitchen, two bedrooms and a pull-out couch. It was walking distance to the mall and The Brisbane Wheel as well as a gorgeous city park and swimming lagoon with a man-made beach. I booked three nights, enough for us to explore the city, and to give everyone a breather from each other, but not so expensive that Clint could claim it broke the budget.

We left that afternoon and swung by Coles to grab groceries for the weekend. We found our condo, parked the Red Rocket in underground parking and it was all hands on deck getting the five of us, several grocery bags, five loaded backpacks and our trail of carry along items, personal items, and pillows up to the fifteenth floor. It was never lost on me how homeless and in disarray we always looked. God forbid we make two or even three trips. Nope, everything had to go up at once! We left the car parked for the weekend and explored the entire city centre by foot. I downloaded a tourist info trail map of the area and we spent the first day exploring the churches and museums. On day two we took the Brisbane ferry across the channel and walked the 5 km trail to the SouthBeach day use area where we ate ice cream and the boys took to the water for a refreshing break from the sweltering heat. It was a great getaway and the first time the five of us had been together just as a family for two months.

After our post-Christmas city break to downtown Brisbane, we returned to my in-laws' house for a few more days before repacking and heading north. We would spend three weeks road-tripping via the coastal town of Tin Can Bay and the city of Rockhampton. Airlie Beach was our final destination, though Cairns was originally our big dream. That would have been another 1,000 km though, and after way too many hours in the Red Rocket, we knew had driven far enough.

Airlie Beach is home to Whitehaven National Park and the Whitsunday Islands, surrounded by the famous Great Barrier Reef. Snorkelling the reef and a day trip out to the Islands was a no brainer for me. *You don't come all this way and not snorkel the reef,* I thought. But Clint's big question was, *how much?* And so, after perusing the tour booths, asking all the questions and collecting all the facts, the negotiations began. A $500 CAD day is a huge hit when your daily budget is $100 CAD and the overall trip budget is already stretched. We couldn't afford many more days like this one. In the end, we booked it and went with the awareness that we might have to turn down some fun opportunities further along.

I had expected difficult things on this trip, like getting tired of each other, feeling uncomfortable, arguing about schoolwork, and losing valuables. But the endless stress and frustration of being over-budget and unable to afford experiences was not something I'd anticipated. I had grandiose dreams of organized tours, dining out, and exploring tourist hot spots. But being a traveller in a tourist world is hard, way harder than I could have imagined. We had to say no *way* more than we could say yes and it wore on everyone. In this case, I couldn't imagine coming home and saying we missed snorkelling the Great Barrier Reef over $500. So we agreed to re-evaluate our finances later, cut costs somewhere else, and booked a single-day tour for the next morning. We were greeted by Skipper Dougie (who kept us in stitches all day with his hilarious sense of humour and comedic presence) and geared up in wetsuits for snorkelling. We climbed aboard our speed boat Big Fury and met the rest of our group; there were about 20 of us in total. Most notably, this was the day we met a couple named Gary and Marlene, who would make another important appearance later in our travels. This was one of our best days out on the water, with Big Fury cutting through the terrifying waves of the Indian Ocean while the wind blew my hair into complete disarray. We learned Rylan was terrified of the ocean and fast boats, he clung to my side and couldn't wait for it to be over. We docked at Whitehaven National Park and hiked for a view of the Pinterest-famous sand swirls, devoured a delicious beach barbecue, and bathed in the sun on the finest, whitest sand I suspect we will ever encounter in our life. Lastly, we enjoyed a float in the bluest, greenest, crystal clear water. We met the island's large and rather angry-looking resident iguana, who raced in and out of our legs like a begging dog, sniffing around tables, awaiting food scraps of any kind. The boys and Gary swam 100 feet out to cartwheel and backflip off of Big Fury into the water, laughing with delight. Whitehaven Beach is unspoiled and as close as I'll get to visiting heaven on earth in my opinion. When it was time to go it took a tugboat worth of effort to pull my reluctant butt back onto Big Fury and I vowed to return one day. When we got home, we chopped fruit and melted chocolate on the stove; our travel-budget version of chocolate fondue, a regular treat for us at home in Canada. It had been a perfect day and we slept like babies that night.

Our epic three-week east coast road trip took us over 3000 kms to some of the most pristine coastline and deserted beaches in the world. We never tired of pulling over and snapping a beach selfie or hitting the waves for an hour. We found waterfalls and freshwater ponds; visited a koala hospital; fed dolphins up close; and spent many many hours hitting up local malls and McDonalds for free Wi-Fi—extremely hard to find in Australia—to catch up with loved ones and book our travel ahead. We braved a terrifying rainstorm with a flash-flood threat in the Red Rocket, one of the only three times I was ever scared during our trip. This stretch of highway had flood markers lining the ditch, letting us know how high the water could possibly get and that it was prone to flash floods, which we weren't that familiar with. We frantically tried to find out what the road conditions were like ahead so we could decide whether we should stop or not. We texted Sheldon, who took pride in being somewhat of a weather nerd, but he was working and never replied. Even in our fear, we felt safer continuing through it, and instead of stopping carried on. About 15 minutes later, the sky broke and the pouring rain stopped. We were in the clear.

Mostly, the trip was ideal. We rode bikes; lounged by the pools at our stays; loaded up on passionfruit and lemon lime Bundaberg sodas; devoured lady finger bananas, and smashed meat pies. In Australia, you don't "eat" meat pies, you "smash" them, which means the same thing. With the exception of an occasional stop for $10 fish and chips, eating out in Australia was extremely expensive. Even McDonalds took a round out of us, so, as in Fiji, treats were few and far between. Eating out came out of necessity and convenience, rarely pleasure. We stayed in furnished apartments with full kitchens and mastered the art of buying the exact amount of groceries we needed for the time that we would be there. We toted around the same God-forsaken ratty and ripped shopping bag of condiments and spices everywhere we went for two months.

Back in Tin Can Bay, we had reconnected via email with old family friends, Len and Jan. We hadn't seen them since they had traveled to Canada 20 years earlier, but my parents were excited for us to call them. Len and Jan were glad to hear from us of course, and welcomed us with open arms. They met us at our rental house the night we arrived in Tin Can Bay. We hugged, introduced them to our boys, exchanged life updates, and recalled old stories. They owned a local cafe and a tourist attraction famous for the small pod of dolphins that swam to their oceanfront cafe shore every morning, year round. People lined up early and paid $5 for a pail of fish, taking turns to stand ankle deep in the waters of the Great

Sandy Strait to feed the dolphins by hand. I had discovered this attraction while looking online but had no idea that Len and Jan were the owners! What a surprise. They bought us breakfast and held places in line for us first thing. As if on cue, 4 beautiful dolphins came gliding in from the sea for their morning feeding. It was another magical experience to add to our list of amazing experiences. Our friends took us for pizza and treated us like Canadian royalty. I was so glad we took the time and made the effort to connect with them. God, His creation, and His people are so good!

We returned to Brisbane just in time to celebrate my nephew Jude's 6th birthday. After another week catching up, and exploring the city some more, it was time to head south. Melbourne had a long list of exciting things waiting for us. First up, The Great Ocean Road!

Australia Part Three

Melbourne was calling our name and we had flights booked just three weeks ahead to Phuket, Thailand, on March 6th. We found a great deal on a one-way car rental to Melbourne; repacked our bags for what felt like the millionth time; gave the caravan and house a final cleaning; and cooked a lovely 'thank you for everything' steak and crab dinner for Clint's family. We said our goodbyes and were off!

Marlene, who we'd met back in Airlie Beach, had got my attention one day when she asked me how our trip was going. I had a pre-programmed response to this question, having continually encountered comments like, '*Wow you're so lucky, what a great education*,' and, '*You must be having so much fun, what an experience.*' All true, but hard to process some days when it wasn't feeling so fun. But my conversation with Marlene in Airlie Beach had tripped me up.

"Wow, that must be so hard. Travel is hard. Good for you guys, but with kids? How are you coping? Do you ever regret it?" Her string of questions came in a single breath.

Interesting I thought. With the biggest sigh of relief I *finally* got to unload.

"It's so hard!" I said. "*Thank you* for asking me that! Really, everyone focuses oh how awesome it is and I feel so guilty sometimes when I find it hard instead of fun. It seems easy to my husband. He handles things differently than I do. Even the kids are doing well. It's mostly me, and it's harder than I thought it would be, and in so many different ways."

It felt joyous to say it out loud and finally feel heard by another human being, another female. The truth was that the kids *were* actually doing awesome. Clint and I remarked proudly and repeatedly on how adaptable the boys were. They just coped and problem-solved and rarely griped. They slept on terrible beds, saw cockroaches, and didn't always have clean or enough clothes. They found the silver lining in the cloud, every time. I felt trapped under the cloud.

It was a little different for Carson. Like his brothers, he reacted well to circumstances of the trip, but unfortunately was struggling emotionally in the bigger picture. He never wanted to come in the first place and his teenaged-self seemed on a mission, over the course of these nine months, to remind us he was *not* happy to be along for the ride, lest we forget. He missed friends and school life, and had recently started an online friendship with a girl from back home. These social ties made it increasingly difficult to keep him connected to us and to the present moment. Carson's free time became a ravenous hunt for Wi-Fi to stay connected to his peers, especially the new girl. For me, social media was a lifeline on the road. I was so thankful for the ability to check in, update our people on our whereabouts, and post photos. But connecting went much further for Carson, becoming a double-edged sword as he lost the ability to separate himself from home, even for just a short while. It was extremely frustrating and became a bone of contention for the rest of the trip. He never came around, even right to the end; another item on my laundry list of disappointments.

Securing a membership with Servas International was something I had worked hard on before we left Canada. It involved a lengthy application and in-person interview. The plan was to use this organization as travellers first, and then use it to host travellers when we returned. Armed with my Letter of Introduction, I fired off multiple email requests looking for members to host us for free during the next portion of our trip. Australia is full of Servas hosts so we didn't expect difficulty, but it turns out not many have room for a family of five. In the end, we heard from two families who graciously agreed to host us: one for two nights just outside of Sydney, and one for three nights in Geelong, near Melbourne. Additionally, we had reconnected online with Marlene and Gary, who we had spent the day with back on Big Fury, and they invited us to stay with them in Melbourne. They purchased blow up beds, tracked down some bedding, and said they couldn't wait to have us!

I messaged Marlene a couple of days before our arrival to check in and make sure everything was still a go, and that's when it got weird. She was at the hospital with her mother-in-law but was evasive about the details and VERY stressed. She had been up for two nights and hadn't been at work all week. I felt terrible imposing on them, but unfortunately, we were unprepared to be anywhere else. Melbourne is extremely expensive on the best of days, we hadn't had time to research a Plan B, and Marlene *insisted* we still come (though with a fair warning that things were stressful at the moment.) Clint and I discussed it at length, and eventually decided not to cancel. I insisted that we would buy our own groceries, keep ourselves busy, and not be a hassle to them whatsoever.

Arriving on their doorstep a couple days later felt uncomfortable to say the least. We had no idea what to expect and both Clint and I had second guessed our decision several times during the drive. Gary was still at work when we arrived but Marlene was home and was as warm and welcoming as anyone could be under the circumstances. She was tired, nervous, and clearly distracted. I'm not sure how much the kids picked up, as we had purposely tried not to say too much. Showing up on the doorstep of near-strangers to spend a weekend was getting to be a normal experience, but it never stopped feeling a little strange. In this case we had only spent three or so hours with our hosts before arriving in their home. But we were there, and we hugged, and Marlene showed us their simple but very comfortable older home. Clint and I were on a blow-up bed in the spare room and they had planned to roll out foamies and another blow-up bed in the living and dining rooms for the boys.

We drank iced tea and all sat in the living room watching the local news which was blaring on the TV. I couldn't help but notice how engulfed Marlene was in the story. The anchor was interviewing some residents from a Melbourne neighbourhood that had heard gunshots a few nights earlier. They had witnessed someone walking up to a neighbour's doorstep and firing a shot into the house, injuring the woman who had answered the door. It was a huge story, and was being considered a drive-by shooting. The suspect was still at large, and the neighbours, needless to say, were on edge. Marlene was mesmerized by the TV, which piqued my spidey-senses. Listening to the details, I noticed that the victim's last name was Smithers—same as our hosts—and that her age sounded close to what Gary's mom could be.

Trying to sound casual, I asked Marlene, "Is that neighbourhood close to here?"

"Yes, it's only a few blocks from here," she replied. "I know it well."

She didn't offer any more information. The news coverage ended and I convinced her to take a nap, saying we were happy to hang out with their sweet cat until Gary got home from work. *Was the shooting victim Gary's mom?!* It would explain the hospital, the stress, and the withholding of details. I panicked. *Who are these people? What are we doing here? Are we crazy staying with people we know nothing about? Could we be in danger?* I ran my little hypothesis past Clint. He shrugged it off. He had missed most of the news story, rolling around the floor with the cat, and generally hadn't been paying attention to anything that was going on. So I prayed and worried on my own, waiting for Gary to get home, thinking maybe I could get the scoop out of him. He made a grand entrance an hour later, showing excitement for us to be there. He high fived the boys, gave us all hugs, turned up the music, and set to work moving furniture and rolling out the beds for the boys. Gary was full of life!

"Wow, what a cool guy," the boys kept saying.

Gary and Clint left for the grocery store to get groceries for dinner; we had decided together on tacos, easy and cheap! As if hosting us for free at his house all weekend wasn't enough, he insisted on buying the groceries for our entire stay. He would not let us pay for *anything*. He cooked dinner and insisted on cleaning up the kitchen himself. He would not let us set foot in the kitchen once the entire weekend. Quite the guy! I wasn't entirely surprised, this same man had swam with the boys back in Airlie Beach and had barrel rolled off the front of our speedboat Big Fury and did 360s into the water, just like a big kid! The boys loved him. Gary and Marlene were about our age, but hadn't had children. They had been married for about 20 years, were well-traveled, and lived very simply. They had nieces and nephews that they loved dearly and appeared to be quite happy with that. I found them intriguing.

Marlene hadn't gotten up by the time we started cooking dinner so I went out on a limb and asked Gary how his mother was feeling.

"She's doing much better, thanks. Out of surgery now and expected to make a full recovery," he said.

"Do you know any details about what happened yet?" I probed, trying not to let on that I had my suspicions, but didn't really know. Gary said they didn't know who it was but that his nephew had been living there after a stint in jail, so police suspected it was a case of mistaken identity. He asked if Marlene had told us and I admitted that I had figured it out from the news story. Thankfully, he found this humorous and I gave myself a pat on the back for my sleuth skills.

Marlene got up shortly after that and I let her know that I had kind of figured out what was going on and we were just going to pray for his mom and that we were sorry that they were going through this. She apologized for the chaos and was quite mortified that this had happened while we were there. She insisted that we were safe and that they had never been through anything like this before. She was very upset with her nephew and had given him strict instructions not to show up at their house at all that weekend.

Marlene walked us down to the train station the next morning and helped us buy our transfer tickets to downtown Melbourne. We had decided to take the train in, venture around on foot for a while, and planned to end up at The Rod Laver Tennis Arena so that Clint could check an item off his bucket list. We had watched the 2017 Australian Open as we travelled the east coast, and it had taken place at Rod Laver Arena. Clint has always been an avid tennis fan, and now we were all along for the ride. All of us had taken an interest in watching Serena Williams and Roger Federer win their matches at this local arena only a month earlier.

We wandered the alleyways and narrow corridors of the downtown core and had lunch at a trendy Mexican restaurant. We discovered a traditional Aussie dessert bar and enjoyed a custard slice on Cake Street in St. Kilda. The boys barrelled through the gigantic mouth of the entrance of Luna Park, taking in a few of the rides. We wandered the oceanfront esplanade on Sunday afternoon, people watching and enjoying the warm temperatures of summer in Victoria. Marlene and Gary continued to spend time at the hospital over the weekend, and we made ourselves at home and ventured out on our own, exploring Melbourne and the surrounding area. Gary's mom made a full recovery and we made a point to stay in touch after we left to keep up to date with the story.

Australian hospitality continued to bless us beyond words. In the years before leaving Canada, in an effort to keep my travel dream alive and well, we had hosted couch surfers and local bands coming through town. We had an open door policy for anyone who needed a place to stay. Our friends and family thought we were crazy but we always enjoyed sharing a meal with new people and hearing their stories. We hosted backpackers from Austria and Germany, and friends travelling through Canada from France. *What's not to love*, I always thought! The humility it takes to traipse my family of five through strangers's homes in foreign countries is hard to put into words. But we had several full-circle moments while we were hosted, being doted on, fed lovely meals and given warm comfortable places to sleep, all with no expectation of anything in return. We were offered good old-fashioned hospitality, just as I had tried to offer so many times back home. These were just some of my many aha God moments.

Those last 3 weeks in Australia provided us with amazing road trip memories. We rested and relaxed, made many new lifelong friends, explored miles and miles of coastline, found trampoline parks (which the kids developed a new passion for), read books, kayaked, and took in local church services everywhere that we could. This became one of my favourite things to do. When you love God you can also find others who do too, anywhere in the world. We were welcomed as family at every church we visited, and I relished in the moments of worship and thoughtfully prepared messages that always spoke to my heart. God was and is so good. He met with me many times during our trip, at church.

One of our last and most meaningful experiences was our journey along the famous Great Ocean Road. We left early Friday morning and spent the day winding along the narrow, edgy coastline of the very southern tip of Australia. It was spectacularly beautiful in several places but the standing ovation goes to the lighthouses, and the crowning sight was the Twelve Apostles which now goes by the Eight Apostles thanks to weather and erosion. The view alone was worth braving the crowds of thousands of tourists with obnoxious selfie-sticks flailing this way and that. Rylan turned 12 that day and will hopefully treasure the stunning photo of himself overlooking the Apostles for years to come. We returned home that night to a special birthday celebration complete with cake and candles, put on by our Servas host family. Australian hospitality never disappoints.

We can thank Beautiful Australia for so many wonderful memories captured in family photos in front of the Sydney Harbour Bridge and the Opera House; splashing in the waves and swimming in waterfalls; kangaroo crossings; and enjoying Bundaberg soda, chicken schnitzel, beer-battered fries (my favourite food of the trip by this point), and Devonshire tea in the afternoon. Clint fell in love with the blue sky. He couldn't get over how nice it was all day, every day. His easy-going and laid-back personality was exaggerated in Australia; he was always positive and embraced discomfort for the character-building opportunity it can be. He loved the break from life and work and crazy schedules that we were always saddled with back home. I was beginning to wonder how on earth we'd get him to go back!

"I could live here," he blurted out one day. " We should move here."

"And do what?" I replied, knowing full well he was thinking with his emotions.

"I don't know. We could buy a business, or work for our family. Sheldon has connections. It's always so nice, the people are amazing."

I, of course, agreed with the sentiment. I loved the idea of a new adventure and something exciting to think about. But being so far from Canada, in my mind, was just *too* far. The plane ride had nearly given me a stroke, the cost of living was atrocious, and we had barely survived the summer heat. The extreme temperatures down under would be comparable to surviving winter in northern Alberta. It would get old fast and soon make us just as miserable as the extreme and prolonged cold had. Braden and Rylan loved Australia but Carson still wanted to play hockey, and getting him to stay would be a nightmare. It was a fun thought, but not practical. Clint continued to bring it up and I continued to shrug it off.

Australia changed us. We grew closer as a family unit, and left with new Aussie friends for life. We loved taking the continent in through fresh Canadian eyes. We'd come to love her, through tasting her food, driving her roads, and meeting her people. She was no longer a mystery, but now completely familiar, a new friend we knew we'd come back to visit one day. Leaving, we missed her already, but Thailand was next on the itinerary and only a short budget flight away.

> **Travel Tip - Use Scoupon! We did everything with coupons and group deals from this website. They are updated daily and offer amazing deals on hotel stays, restaurants, tours and activities. We saved so much money using Scoupon. I paid $50 CAD for $200 meal credit at a Brazilian restaurant in downtown Brisbane. The four of us ate as much as we could but were tapped out at $150. It was totally worth it.**

Blog Post: March 2017

Thailand has welcomed us warmly, no surprise there. After a long day of flying and airport-hopping we arrived late Sunday night to the sweaty, sticky heat that we had been glad to leave behind in Brisbane.

After negotiating a taxi (and getting ripped off, but we were too tired to care) we jumped in for the ride of our lives through winding bumpy roads and the smells of third world Phuket. We buzzed past markets and food stalls, with music pounding through the air, as well as sirens and the sounds of thousands of scooters and motorbikes. Someone once described Thailand to me as "full-on," and they were correct! Full-on it was.

Our hostel was nothing short of a series of challenges we faced with a 'come on, we can do this' attitude. The extremely steep broken ceramic tile staircase; the dark halls; the hot and sweaty room with no windows. Yes, a private bathroom if that's what you call a shower with a toilet in a stall. At least we have enough giant beds, or so I had thought. But they are as hard as bricks, hence the two massages I've had this week. (I am way too old for this.) And yes, I knew exactly what we were getting. I was hoping to be surprised in a good way, like maybe the pictures and reviews online lied.

The location, though, was fantastic! Turns out the Old Phuket District is being revitalized (hence the constant construction outside of our door) and it is appealing to old and young alike for it's heritage buildings, history, photography, and the many cute and trendy coffee shops and eateries that were mere steps away from our hostel. It was a very exciting place to call home for the week. We toughed out the room and thoroughly enjoyed our surroundings. We ate some of the best, and by far cheapest, food of the whole trip. Finally, we revelled in the lavish, incredibly fast, and free Wi-Fi! Lord knows we've needed it!

Thursday had me and Clint venturing out to Patong Beach without the kids after they begged and pleaded to stay back. Apparently they are tired of the beach. (No comment.) So, after laying down the rules, deciding how far they could go in search of food, off we went, leaving them for the day in the dungeon of the room we called our temporary home. We rode in the rickety, open air back of a truck that Phuket calls the city bus. It cost 30 baht which is about $1.25 CAD and we made it to the beach alive, along with the other 40 Thai's that were crammed in with us. As it turned out, after our bus experience (which was worse on the way back, believe it or not) and seeing Patong Beach for what it really is, an overpacked, loud, smelly, garbage-strewn and over-priced tourist trap, we were glad the kids stayed home.

For this and for many other reasons I am continually thankful for the online travel groups that I have been a part of for years. They educate me about where to go and stay, and where not to, I'd heard Patong Beach was a no-go, but I just had to pop by to see for myself. Good call, travel friends! And good call, kids! Thank God we didn't end up there all week, dungeon room in Phuket Town or not. The experience also left Clint and I thankful that we are on the same page as travellers. Tourist stuff doesn't appeal to either of us. We both appreciate the authentic areas that we visit, away from the madness, into the heart of the back streets and local eateries, even if it means giving up some amenities and comforts.

We did a lot this week. We had $11 CAD massages (twice), devoured hundreds of $2 CAD fresh fruit smoothies, and haggled for knock-off clothing. Clint didn't do too badly, paying $13 CAD for a t-shirt and tank top. He's not satisfied though. Next time he's going for the jugular and aiming for $12. I'll be in the background with my currency app, reminding him that the 100 baht he's haggling over is in fact only $3.75 CAD so we're probably good! Call it a day fella. We even went to the dentist and a cat cafe.

This week has been a real experience for us, though I would be remiss not to mention that Braden suggested we could have 'eased' them into Thailand. Like maybe we could have stayed somewhere nice first before settling into the dungeon. Good call Braden. Sorry about your luck this time! And there you have it, our first week in Thailand, in a nutshell. I don't think there is a side street or back street we haven't ventured down in the lovely Phuket Town! Tomorrow we'll be heading 20 min south to Rawai, a sleepy seaside village on Naiharn Beach for the week. I'm ready to ditch the dungeon, do some laundry, and have a pool! In the meantime, time flies and we're having fun. Tummies and health are holding up for everyone, not one complaint there. Kids are still missing home life but that will return soon enough!

CHAPTER 4

Thailand

We landed in Phuket Town, Thailand in the early evening of Monday, March 6th after a frantic and confusing rental car drop-off in Melbourne and a non-eventful budget flight. We had a layover in Kuala Lumpur, Malaysia where we scarfed down airport Laksa noodle bowls, and the kids hunted down McDonalds. We debated whether an airport layover can be considered a country stop, and it was judged 4-1 that it could be. I was the 1. Unless you actually see the country, it doesn't count in my books.

Arrivals into new places had now taken on a familiar routine. The goal was to get our bags; find Wi-Fi; locate and haggle for transportation if not previously arranged; find sim cards; find currency; and find food. But, we'd learned to take what we could get, in no particular order. In this case, we arrived in Thailand tired and hungry, and being accosted by sweltering heat and impending nightfall. The idea of sorting out airport transportation, with aggressive vendors all touting to be the cheapest (in broken English), and trying to calculate the exchange proved to be too much. We spent way too much money and took the first guy that would take all five of us. We sped off, crammed like sardines piled on top of each other, with luggage tied down this way and that. Our driver spoke no English, and took a quick stop at his workplace, pretending he wanted to understand where we were going. When in reality, his sales agent came out to the car to try to sell us expensive tours. We declined, and he suddenly seemed to know where we were headed and sped off again while we silently wondered if we had made a mistake. In just those 45 minutes Thailand became a serious assault on the senses, every one of them. The noise and smells of pollution and cigarette smoke; the occasional wafting of sewage; the garbage; the food stalls and never ending 7/11's; families of six piled high on street bikes; and the screeching of brakes and engines as we all arrived at the lights together, just to take off again in no particular or safe order. There were no helmets, no car seats, not even baskets. Thailand comes alive at night and she was just waking up when we arrived. It was chaos, absolute and utter, beautiful and interesting chaos with the pounding of music and drinking in the streets. *Please let our hotel be nice, even just decent,* I pleaded silently with God.

We finally arrived and packed our luggage and five free water bottles up two flights of rickety, broken-tiled stairs to a dark room. We attempted to settle in for the night. It was a large room, and free of cockroaches (thank God), and had a single-stall bathroom with a shower head over the toilet. It had good Wi-Fi and really good air conditioning, but it was a dungeon and that's what we referred to it as from then on... *the dungeon*. The dungeon was our home for five nights. The beds were rock hard and came with only a sheet and one flat pillow for each of us. There were no windows either, but who's complaining for $35 CAD per night? On our second night, a very large group of obnoxious and loud young people arrived down the hall around 3:00 am. Some were laughing, some were arguing, and some were drunk, but none quiet. After a frustrating hour of trying to ignore the madness, I hollered down the hall with my angry mom scowl, which sent them apologizing into their rooms. I laid awake wondering what $45 per night might have got us.

The daylight brought new excitement to our trip. We ventured out and explored our neighbourhood, Old Phuket Town, which turned out to be quite the highlight. The kids found macchiatos and pancakes in the cutest, trendiest quaint cafe next door for less than $5 CAD which was exhilarating after the penny-pinching and corner-cutting we had adjusted to in Fiji and Australia. The cafe became our schoolwork spot, and I spent many hours there researching what we would do with the rest of our time in Thailand over cheap, delicious coffee. Thailand might have been a culture shock, leaving us uncomfortable a time or two, but it also gifted us cheap massage heaven and a food fest like no other. We ate crepes and bananas with ice cream for lunch, and smoothies whenever we wanted, all beautifully plated with tropical flowers and adornments. Clint's new favourite dish was Massaman curry (slow cooked beef and tender potatoes in a rich, fragrant, spicy curry), and we also discovered we loved pineapple rice boats, pork fried basil, and green tea with churros. My all time favourite was Khao Soi, a dish that originated in Chiang Mai in Northern Thailand and is a pork ball soup piled high with purple onions, lime, and crunchy noodles. Thailand was a feast for our food senses and most of us were happy to never come home. Carson stuck to burgers, or any American he could find. No rice, no noodles, no soup. Just fries and burgers. He continued to sulk his way through Phuket and onwards, missing the beat on his never-ending search for Wi-Fi. He explored with us, but rarely enthusiastically and usually with some sort of a pout on. We carried on.

We passed on expensive town or island tours and stuck close to home, catching rides to anywhere and everywhere on cheap tuk tuk rides or the local bus. I had planned on day tripping over to Patong one day that week, a cheap one hour bus ride from Phuket. However, when the day arrived, I discovered the kids were tired from walking and had apparently grown tired of the beach since Australia. I was reluctant to let them stay, but after some thoughtful negotiating we decided that Clint and I would go without them. We left with careful and specific instructions, to stay in contact with us via Wi-Fi, where they could go and when, and how they would get food. When everyone was clear, Clint and I ventured off on our own for the day.

It was literally one of our first times away from the kids in *months*. We had a nice afternoon exploring Patong but discovered quickly that we had chosen wisely to not actually stay there. It was loud and expensive, the beach was so packed with people that we could barely find a place to lay our towel, and the water was murky. Being a tourist trap, it was party central, and there was garbage everywhere. So much garbage. We were quite happy when it was time to head back to our dungeon. The kids had started texting and anxiously awaited our return. We somehow missed the 4:00 pm bus, or possibly misunderstood our questionable pickup instructions completely, a regular occurrence while travelling. We ended up catching a ride on the last bus of the day, which happened to collect every last worker from that area heading back to Phuket. Just when I thought we could not possibly pack one more person into that crazy school bus, we'd stop and grab one more. Then another. And then another. People were hanging out the windows and off the back, the engine was dragging and groaning, the driver could barely shift from gear to gear without slapping us all into each other, and we hadn't even begun the long and windy, painfully slow climb up the hill. It made the small mountain that separates Patong from Phuket Town feel like Mount Everest. Our day away was turning sour and I started to slip into familiar panicky doubt, wondering if we had made yet another mistake. I returned to pleading with God: *Just get us home to our babies.* I was suddenly regretting leaving them alone all day.

Imagine for a moment.

Three cute blonde gingers wandering around busy Phuket alone all day. I knew Carson likely went off on his own regardless of our instructions, and the other two were naive and would be potentially careless, again, regardless of our instructions. They're boys, and by now fairly comfortable with their surroundings. In Thailand! The sex trafficking capital of the world! I lost complete control of my thoughts. It was feeling like the worst and most irresponsible decision we could have possibly made. I envisioned having to call home, saying one is missing. We left them alone for the day. *YOU WHAT*???? I heard back. It was an awful situation that I had zero control of. The mind does strange and complicated things when it is in an anxious state. It imagines hypothetical situations and catastrophizes them. That's what my mind began to do, and I was fully aware of it. If it were easy to just *choose* to think positively and rationally, I would have. But I couldn't, and so I didn't, but I sure tried. Clint never said a peep. He gazed out the window, probably just enjoying the scenery.

We eventually made it back to town. Without really knowing how to specify where we were getting off, we got dropped off near a mall we recognized but had to still walk blocks to get back to the kids. They had nothing to report except that they had stayed together but snuck out beyond our permitted boundary so they could get chips and pop from a 7/11. Nothing happened of course, in Thailand or anywhere else we visited. Maybe we were as completely as safe as I did feel originally, so it is strange to revisit the experience in memory and have different feelings. I know we were covered in prayer before we left and the whole time we were away, and for that I am thankful; we all returned alive and well. After the recurrence of anxiety while we were apart, of course I was thrilled to be safely together again. It bothered me that anxiety appeared to be creeping into my mind and life, a big deal for a Type A personality like myself, who typically has a rational and non-emotional outlook and the ability to remain in complete control. It was difficult for me to come to terms with and even more difficult for Clint and the kids to understand. I was the one that wanted this trip, so why couldn't I keep it together when things got rough? I had no answers, I was just left uncomfortably observing myself, taking notes about my mental state.

Our next hotel stay couldn't have come at a better time.

I asked the guy who checked us in, "Why is the hotel named *Again at Naiharn Beach*?"

He replied in adorable broken English, "Well we hope you love it and then return to stay with us again and again and again."

I chuckled to myself. I was learning to enjoy how creative the Thai people can be with the English language. Old Phuket Town was lovely, historic, and only our second foray into the Third World which we were getting well adjusted to. Personally though, I was beyond done with rock-hard beds and showering over a toilet bowl. At the Again at Naiharn Beach Hotel we were greeted with passionfruit drinks delivered to our door, separate bedrooms (a welcome relief to Clint and I for obvious reasons,) a beautiful rock wall shower in the bathroom, a free beach shuttle, and free coffee and breakfast every morning. Our room was lovely but rustic, surrounding a beautiful and clean turquoise-blue pool area, and cost a whopping $65 CAD per night. Goodbye dungeon! We wasted no time hitting the beach, renting lounge chairs for $3 per day, and splurging on candied pineapple and apple pears. The kids bounced around in the waves while I floated and sun tanned. It was glorious and it finally felt like a vacation from our world of travel. Carson joined us occasionally, but chose instead to hike the 3 km to the beach instead of taking the shuttle with us. He was turning into a Forest Gump long haul walker of sorts. His new shtick was that he was tired of the beach, didn't like the ocean, and didn't like the heat. So he wandered around aimlessly, earbuds plugged constantly into his teenage ears, returning only when he was ready, usually for food. Generally we let him be, resigning ourselves to rolling our eyes and wishing he would just get over his issues. On occasion, when I had had enough of his pouty, negative ways I would have a yelling, crying meltdown and let him know he was wrecking everything, begging him to stop being so selfish. He would cry and yell back that he was miserable and depressed and *please* could we just send him home? He never wanted this. Well, neither did I.

This was not the dream. *Dear God, was this a mistake? Please tell me we have not wrecked the boys' lives and futures on a selfish whim of mine to fulfill a dream that could have waited until they were grown and gone.*

Of course you haven't, God would whisper back.

This is what teenagers do, they wreak havoc on common sense. They somehow turn unconditional love and devotion, and hopes and dreams of bigger things and a promising enlightened future into abuse against them. They are given the world and it's never enough, it's not right. But we did what we do best as a family. We found our way back to each other. Hours later, Carson would apologize profusely, promising to do and be better. He would pray for a new attitude, and I loved him still, and always, and all over again, fresh. We'd start over until next time. Next time returned, many times over.

Clint turned 42 in Thailand, but I don't even think he realized it was coming! Days ran into the next with little to no agenda let alone anything major to think about or remember. I reminded him the morning of and we went out for his favourite Massaman curry dish for dinner, splurging on mango sticky rice for dessert. When in Thailand, you eat what the Thais eat! Not that a piece of Safeway birthday cake wouldn't have been nice, but it was nowhere to be found!

We had heard reports from various people regarding the business that we had sold. The owners had, after all, moved into our home so we did hear from them regularly. Unfortunately, the main, seasoned staff member that we had left to assist the new owners' transition had decided to quit two weeks before Christmas, leaving them (a shipping company) with only one remaining staff member to manage the busiest two weeks of the year. We felt disappointed and frustrated on their behalf, but were silently thankful that we were a world away and didn't have to worry about getting involved. Not that they would have expected that, but I'm sure the help was badly needed.

Two weeks in Thailand flew by and little did we know that the adventure was just getting started! As part of my million hours of research, I discovered *12Go Asia*, an online transport company run by Americans but based in, and focused on, Thailand. What a God-send they turned out to be. With their help, and a lot of careful consideration about cost, safety, and where else we wanted to visit, I planned the rest of our time in Thailand. We took a taxi back to Phuket Town to catch a sketchy, 4-hour long bus ride to Surat Thani where we boarded an overnight train to Bangkok. Thanks to 12GoAsia, our tickets were waiting for us at the bus terminal and the transfers all came together perfectly. From there we planned to meet up with our church youth group to drop Carson off, explore for a day or two, and then head east to Hua Hin Thailand where I booked a glorious 10-day stay at the 5-star Marriott Hua Hin, *all free on credit card points*! Everyone napped soundly on the bus while I stayed awake and alert, watching our belongings and making sure the sleepy driver stayed awake. Sleepy drivers are common in Thailand. We learned that their schedules are overbooked, crammed with long trips, and sometimes the drivers go without sleeping for days, just to make an extra buck. It would not be the last time we had to keep our eyes peeled on our driver which was highly unsettling. No one spoke a word of English so it always felt like a hope and a prayer that we would actually arrive where we were supposed to, let alone on time.

About an hour into our bus ride we took a quick roadside stop for treats and drinks and to use a washroom, which was an old rusty toilet bowl with a jug in a bucket of murky water to wash it down. Somehow I figured it out and thanked God for wet wipes. The driver spoke enough English to understand where we wanted to stop. We were pleasantly surprised when he dropped us off smack in front of the train station, and we didn't have to walk or taxi there as we had planned to. He pulled up, gave us a whistle, snapped his fingers, dropped our mile-high stack of backpacks in the middle of the road, and off he went. We collected our tickets from the reservation office without hiccups, enjoyed another nice Thai meal, grabbed some trip treats from a 7-11, and waited for our overnight train for Bangkok which arrived right on time!

After stashing our bags wherever we could, our train car steward made his way around to help us get comfortable and make our beds up for the night. He even offered us breakfast for our 6:00 am arrival time. We snapped photos of each other in our bunks before going out to tour a few other train cars and acquaint ourselves with squat toilets for the first time since arriving in Thailand.

No sooner had we changed into our jammies, climbed into our bunks, and attempted to adjust to the aggressive swaying and loud banging noise of train travel, did Braden call out to me from behind his curtain, looking greener than the Grinch.

"Mom, I don't feel very good,"

"*Crap,*" I thought out loud.

I hustled him down the corridor to an open washroom (thank God) where he quickly learned how to squat, rinse, and then puke his motion sickness away. I was outside the door, guarding it for dear life and praying that he would be ok and figure it all out. We hadn't covered squat toilets in our pre-Thailand talks. We had prepared them for the possibilities of seeing old white men with Thai girls, massage parlours, prostitution, and lady boys, but not squat toilets.

About 10 minutes later Braden staggered out, all cleaned up and feeling better. I rubbed his head down with peppermint oil and gave him a Gravol. He slept like a baby and woke up fine. Our first overnight train trip was a successful, enjoyable, and non-eventful experience, minus the old Thai guy who made a point of stopping to shake each of the boys hands, clicking his tongue on the roof of his mouth as he did. He wanted to know their ages and names, and he made off after a few minutes of us refusing him that information. I have no idea to this day what the tongue clicking was all about.

Bangkok was nuts! We are talking Nadi, Fiji, times 100. Loud, horns, smog, a billion people everywhere, sewer smell, meat markets and mayhem. No sooner had we gotten our luggage off the train, taxi drivers started yelling prices at Clint and within seconds we were being rammed into the back of a small beat up car while our luggage was tied down with tarp straps, hanging out the back. For 900 baht, we raced through the busy city streets of Bangkok, Thailand as the city was just beginning to awake. Skytrains zipped overhead, and motorbikes zoomed by us, piled high with families and babies without helmets. This was the first of a couple of overnight trips that I had planned, but this being our first I learned a few things. One—it really sucks to show up to a hotel at 7:00 am when check-in isn't until 3pm or 4pm. And two—I'm unable to sleep on these overnight adventures so the first thing I need to do when we arrive is hit the hay. This doesn't always suit my family who typically sleep well wherever they are, and arrived at our destinations fresh and ready to explore. *Thank God* for more free hotels paid for with points, and first-class service for being a Gold member. There was a loud, rowdy group of Aussies waiting in the lobby and I overheard them being told their rooms weren't going to be ready until the afternoon. We were given early check-in priority and ushered to our beautiful, comfortable rooms. After a good rest for me, some good Wi-Fi use for the guys, and a delicious breakfast buffet, our hotel concierge insisted on us using the Skytrain. For small-city foreigners, that felt extremely intimidating, but we put our big-people travel pants on and trekked to the ticket booth. We successfully used Bangkok's Skytrain system to visit its famous flea markets, where we stocked up on cheap bags, and knock-off Nikes, t-shirts, and ankle socks for a pittance. We had an exciting reunion with our church youth team the next morning, got caught up on all the latest gossip from home, sent Carson on his way to volunteer in the local communities and churches with his friends, and returned back to the hotel to pack up again for our trip east. The Mariott Hua Hin was calling our name!

The Mariott Hua Hin was the nicest hotel we have ever stayed in, or may ever stay in again. We were welcomed with delicious-smelling cold cloths for our faces; cold heaven-sent passionfruity welcome drinks; valet service; and a glorious upgrade to the 'pool entry' rooms for being valued Gold members. Who knew using our credit card for all those years would be such a pay off! Our room was beachfront, the kids had access to club activities and waterslides, and there was a mall within walking distance for eating and necessities. We loaded up our little hotel fridge with breakfast muffins, yogurt and coffee, and walked back over twice a day for lunch and dinner. It was delightful. We read books and floated on the lazy river right from our room. The boys used the waterslide, rode their first pony on the beach, and hit the Thailand waves yet again. We slept late and I spent hours continuing to piece together the rest of our trip. We heard from Carson via Wi-Fi daily; he was having a good time, and, other than a couple of days sick with a cold, was having a great time. We relaxed into the luxury of long walks on the beach, chocolates and exotic fruit delivered to our room daily, and many more cheap massages. We had our entire load of laundry washed, pressed and folded for $8 CAD!

There wasn't a lot going on culturally in Hua Hin—it's mostly a resort town for Bangkokers—but about 3 days in we heard about an elephant rescue organization where we could volunteer for a few hours, bathing and caring for orphaned elephants and learning all about them. It was a small organization, and perhaps a bit of a gimmick, but it was our first time we'd had the opportunity to get up close to such majestic gentle giants. We got some real, live elephant hugs, took some great photos, left a donation, and had an overall enjoyable experience.

Rylan took some interest in learning to cook local Thai food so after some research and reading reviews online, I found a great local cooking academy. We got picked up by the cooking school chef just outside the doors of our hotel and the three of us spent the day perusing the outdoor market to gather our vegetables, fruits and spices. We chopped and ground spices to a paste, and carved peppers into flowers. Our meal was complete with pineapple rice, veggie spring rolls, penang chicken curry, and mango sticky rice. It was Thai food heaven! Our chef even had me call the other two to come and eat with us when the food was ready, and we had leftovers for days. This was such an unexpected treat and another highlight of our trip.

I had previously spent days researching local volunteer organizations and attempting to find places to give of our time. Unfortunately, that desire generally went unfulfilled. The volunteer industry is a bit of a gong-show and the only options I could find involved spending hundreds, or even thousands of dollars to be able to volunteer with local charities. So I was pleasantly surprised to find an international church just down the road from our hotel that ran a Children's home. It was run by a British man, so I knew we wouldn't have a language issue. We traipsed down for church one Sunday, hot and sticky as usual. We enjoyed a wonderful Thai church service, met lots of people, and were invited back to the Children's home that night for dinner and a baptism service in the ocean. We gathered with a colorful and eclectic group of locals and expats around a huge table laid out with plates and platters of the most delicious Thai dishes. We met Dave, a single guy in his mid-40's from the UK who chose to retire early in Thailand. He spent his days helping with church and the care home, an older Swiss couple who were the Pastors/spiritual leaders of the home, many younger Thai women, and others. They were warm and welcoming and there was enough food for us plus about a hundred more. We sauntered down to the oceans edge as a group to witness the water baptism of a couple from church, sang songs while someone played guitar, and just revelled unanimously in the Glory of God. I was so content. *By the Grace of God,* I reflected with a smile on my face and happiness in my heart. *By the Grace of God.*

Ten days came and went like a flash and before we knew it we were loading up into yet another taxi and heading back to Bangkok.

I had a bad gut feeling immediately. Our driver showed up with bloodshot eyes, looking buzzed and I SWEAR I found an empty booze bottle on the floor in the back seat. He wasted no time reaching speeds up to 130 km/hr, and dozing off at the wheel. Of course Clint was up front beside him, but I could see what was happening from the back. Within half an hour Braden, who is known to be particularly observant and sensitive, tapped me and in full panic mode let me know what I already knew, this guy was either wasted or running on days with no sleep. I communicated to Clint from the back seat that we need to pull over *as soon as possible* and that this guy needed a slap. We stopped at a 7-11 and discussed cutting our losses and finding a new ride, not an easy option still two and a half hours from our destination, in the middle of nowhere in 35 degree heat. So Clint, in full dad-mode, laid into the driver and let him know that he'd better wake up and stop speeding. We were scared and poor Braden wouldn't even get back in the car. He was weeping with emotional overwhelm, and thinking we were definitely about to die out here on this crazy road with this crazy driver. It took a quick prayer with him and all the coaxing in the world to get him back in the car. I didn't relax for one second for the rest of that trip, wishing I had stuck to my guns and kept the 12GoAsia driver that I had originally booked, and not given in to Clint's idea to hire this cheaper guy we found on the side of the road. I learned later that it is important in Thailand to book with a reputable online company with good reviews only because some drivers cram days of driving back and forth to Bangkok on little to no sleep and that accidents are common. I think we all kissed the ground of the Sheraton Bangkok when we finally arrived safe and sound. Lesson learned: lots of the time, Mama knows best! We had another free three-night stay at the Royal Orchid Sheraton on the Chao Phraya River. We unpacked our bags, sorted out our adventures for the next few days, and booked our flights to Dubai.

Bangkok will be forever known to us as *'Scam City.'* It was a fairly harmless scam in the end, mostly just a waste of our day and a couple hundred baht which is nothing, but it makes a great story. We were heading on foot like usual to find a tuk tuk which was supposed to take us to one of Bangkok's largest Buddhist temples. Instead, we were interrupted by a local who suggested we try the green "government" tuk tuks which were much cheaper and known only to the locals. He flagged one down for us, privately instructed the driver in Thai, and sent us on our way. He ended up touring us through a series of temples, a shop that sold custom-made suits, and tourist stops that were all in cahoots with each other to get us to spend our rich-white-people big-bucks! I remember standing as a family in this two story sea of custom made suits, wondering why on earth we were there. What do we want with custom suits? It was so confusing, yet no alarm bells rang. The temple before this stop had rolled out the red carpet and let us know that it was our lucky day!

It was "sale day" at the tailors, only happens one day a year! he said. *It was written in the stars for us to be in Bangkok on this special day!*

We shot each other "what do we do" looks? This was of course after he had told us a long and ridiculously animated story of how this was the largest and oldest temple in Thailand.

It doesn't look old and large, I thought. Still, there were no red flags, just confusion. We were so naive. We weren't interested in any of it of course, but in the end had a fairly good tour of Bangkok and were returned to our hotel as promised, with only the waste of a morning under our belt. Our concierge had a good laugh at our little adventure and said, "Welcome to Bangkok, the most famous scam out there!"

We started out again the next day, on high alert for another scam. We took yet another crazy, over-capacity, bottomed-out mode of Thai transportation. This time it was an ancient riverboat that looked like it was ready to explode, heading upstream to the Wat Pho Buddhist Temple and The Temple of the Reclining Buddha. This ride did not help with Rylan's fear of water; he was terrified and convinced we were going to drown. It was trudging up river the same way that dreadful bus trudged up that hill to Phuket. Truthfully, I was only convinced otherwise myself once we actually made it ashore. We had a great day touring the Buddhist temples, and browsing flower markets. We ended at Asiatique, a fantastic modern open-air shopping market, where we reunited with Carson and had a great dinner with his team. We returned to the hotel and prepared to leave Thailand the next morning.

Bangkok was majestic and exciting but we were ready for our next adventure. So after a month in Thailand, six hotels, an overnight train and bus trip, we set our alarms for 4:00 am, accidentally slept in, and frantically threw our bags together in a panic to catch our taxi to the airport. Dubai and the Arabian desert heat were calling our names! In our scramble we left one of Clint's best Adidas hiking shoes with custom made insoles, Carson's Bauer hoodie, and yet another airplane neck pillow behind. Such is life on the road.

Travel Tip #1 - Use 12GoAsia whenever needed. They were hands down, by far the most economical and practical way to piece together car rentals, bus and train trips and short domestic flights. Their drivers won't fall asleep at the wheel!

#2- Try to avoid elephant riding tours. These gentle giants are seldom treated well, they are taken on long haul trips without proper back support nor nourishment. Try to focus on elephant sanctuaries where they will let you bathe and love on these precious creatures.

#3- Use Trip Advisor and find a good Thai cooking class. They are reasonably priced and great fun.

CHAPTER 5

Dubai

We arrived in Abu Dhabi, collected our luggage, and made our way to Dubai on a luxury coach supplied by the airline. What a difference the dry desert heat was, reminding me of the summers at home. Dubai was hotter than hot but not humid; we badly needed a change from the constant sweating we've been doing for months now. We continued to bask in the glory of free hotels from our credit card rewards. We stayed at the lovely four-star Sheraton on Dubai Creek in Old Dubai. It didn't take long for the kids to spot Tim Hortons—yes, Dubai has many—and the heaps of luxury cars blowing by our luxury coach! First impressions included very clean streets, some areas that looked older than I expected, newer more modern areas, higher skyscrapers than we've ever seen in our life, less traffic and people than we expected, and overall a super-fun vibe. People were lovely and kind everywhere, and spoke great English. Dubai had the biggest mish-mash of cultures and languages, and it took two days for us to figure out who the native Arabs were. Everyone lives very amicably together and crime is reportedly nearly non-existent.

We checked in to adjoining rooms and began to plan out our quick three-day stay in Dubai. Our first outing of the weekend was a four-hour Big Bus tour of the entire city, including a stop at the Dubai Mall and a zippy tour to the top of the Burj for Braden and Clint; a drive by the first and oldest Spice Souk of Dubai where gold and spices can be bought in bulk; and a visit to the Dubai Museum, right after our quick jaunt into

Tim Hortons for Iced Capps of course! We also squeezed in a stop for lunch at the famous Jumeirah Beach. Dubai is such an eclectic mix of new and old, beach and desert, religious and secular, filthy rich and pay cheque to pay cheque (who we know exist as they were driving our taxis all weekend). Our last stop of the tour was Dubai Mall which is a sight to be seen and proudly claims status as the largest mall in the world. Either way, its four beautiful floors hold over a thousand high-end stores, markets, fountains, and food courts, as well as an ice rink, an aquarium, and a theme park! It's also home to the Burj Khalifa, currently the tallest tower in the world. You couldn't pay me enough to go up, but Clint and Braden had a fantastic afternoon on the 125th floor, exploring the city from the clouds and taking heaps of photos! While I was having a quick lunch with Rylan at the food court, a text popped in from Clint. He was showing me panoramic photos of the city from the top. It was breathtaking and I couldn't grasp how high they actually were. Talk about a once in a lifetime opportunity! We reunited just before dinner and headed out to the mall's outdoor restaurant galleria where the world renowned dancing fountains come to life. If you've ever been to Vegas and enjoyed the fountains at the Bellagio, these made those look like a penny fountain. The dancing fountains are plumbed into a thirty-acre lake with powerful jets covering an area of two football fields. Every 30 minutes, the colourful and dancing jets come to life by swooping and swaying, synchronized to music such as Thriller by Michael Jackson; a completely free and spellbinding show. It was absolutely magical and mesmerizing.

We returned to our hotel, completely exhausted and far too tired to go out and find cheap food, so after rooting around online, I found a 24-hour, free food-delivery service, chose a restaurant on our price point and voila! Delicious Indian curries were at our door thirty minutes later. Welcome to Dubai!

The next morning, we took an Uber over to the mall which was supposed to be our meeting point for the sand dunes tour we'd booked through Groupon. After at least an hour of running the mall end to end and repeatedly calling the tour operator (who spoke in terrible broken English) to try to figure out where this ridiculous meeting point was, we finally discovered them waiting across the street. We made our departure time by mere moments! The bus was hot and sweaty without air conditioning, which of course wasn't mentioned in the reviews. We were crammed in like sardines and the trip was *long,* but overall we had fun and it was a good value for the price. Once there, we piled into 4x4s, and barely had time to get our seat belts secured before the music got cranked and we were told to hang on for the ride of our lives. We crashed through sand dunes, flew over rolling hills, swerved into sand banks and flailed back and forth while I seriously wondered if we were going to die right there in the Dubai desert. I screamed, and the boys laughed and howled, sometimes nervously but mostly just taking it all in with glee. We slammed to a stop outside of a large colourful tent that was surrounded by camels and men awaiting our arrival. They placed headdresses on our heads without asking and then basically demanded 50 Dirham ($17 CAD). Clint was annoyed and almost refused but the kids thought they looked funny and we all agreed to wear them just for fun. We wandered around aimlessly, wondering what exactly the plan was. Dinner and drinks were included, along with a few activities but most things cost extra money and we were promptly notified the drinks weren't free until dinner at 5:00 pm. It was only 3:00 pm… sigh. The boys weren't interested in riding a camel. The animals smelled absolutely wretched and looked like they hadn't eaten in months, but I wasn't going to leave the desert without riding one. Besides, I wanted to get my money's worth on the Groupon package. So Clint and I went for a short, photo-worthy traipse around the grounds on an old, crusty, cranky camel. We all got henna tattoos and dressed up in Arab clothes and posed for goofy photos, which were so fun to post on Facebook later for our friends and family to see. 5:00 pm finally rolled around so we chose a table and sat around on brightly coloured blankets on the ground. Our evening was filled with delicious and unique Middle Eastern food, music, belly dancing, fire dancing, and hours of fun. We loaded back onto the bus under the desert stars and made our way back to the bright city lights of Dubai.

We disembarked, said good-bye and started back across the street to the mall when Clint realized he didn't have his phone.

"I left it on the bus!" he shouted.

"It's still in the parking lot," I said frantically. "But it's starting to leave… hurry!"

Like in a scene from a movie, Clint darted across four lanes of busy Dubai traffic, waved the bus down as it was proceeding through the light, raced to the back of the bus, and found his phone sitting on the seat exactly where he had left it. In another minute that bus would have been long gone. We all cheered and laughed hysterically as he raced back through traffic, waving his phone in the air.

We absolutely LOVED Dubai and the boys vowed to return one day. We felt completely safe at all times and welcomed as tourists. With it being such a new city, and so overwhelmingly multicultural, it was left to our imagination who the locals were and who was considered a tourist in the first place. It was such an interesting dichotomy with traditional garb, like burqa-covered women, blending well somehow with the modern, semi-clad western-influenced women. It just *works*, which is not to dismiss the heavy influence of Islam and Sharia law that is clearly present. As an outsider looking in, it appears to blend well. I spent hours in the Dubai Mall food court watching, learning, and admiring the variety and dynamics of women with their families present around me, living the same life that I am, yet so differently. Even in the traditional conservative Muslim families before my eyes, men still fed and carried their babies and held their wives' hands. The wives, covered head to toe with only their eyes visible, toted Victoria Secret and Lululemon shopping bags. It was eye-opening and interesting and left me pondering everything I thought I knew about Muslim life in the Middle East.

Monday morning came in the blink of an eye. While I packed up and cleaned our room, Clint zipped over to the laundry business where we had left our ever-growing load of dirty clothes. We had left strict instructions not to press anything because of the outrageous extra charge; we weren't in Thailand anymore after all! Clint grabbed the clothes in a hurry, paid in Dirham, and hailed a taxi to rejoin us at the hotel. We quickly grabbed another Uber and headed for the cruise port. It wasn't until we chatted later and did a quick currency calculation that we realized that they had in fact pressed our clothes and our laundry had cost us $80 CAD! It was too late, and so frustrating, and another reminder that life on the road is sometimes complicated and regularly annoying. We brushed it off and labeled it as what it would humorously become money mistake number one of three.

The ship was huge and stunning, and excitement was in the air. Carson had returned to us from Thailand with a touch of the flu and a cold. The day before we boarded I was starting to feel it in my throat and lungs, but for fear of being discovered by the ship's nursing staff, I checked off all of the healthy boxes on the ship intake form. And so we hit the open seas in the afternoon, on Monday April 24th, heading to our first port: Muscat, Oman!

Travel Tip - Use Groupon! It was loaded with competitively priced group tours, cheaper Big Bus tour options and many more great itinerary ideas. Read the reviews and enjoy the savings!

Blog Post: April 2017

There are several awesome things about a sixteen day cruise. This time, for us, it was that since we spent the first half sick in bed, we still had a week to have fun once we got better!

The bad news is that we can now add spending almost $300 CAD to see a ship doctor to our list of life experiences. The good news is that we all recovered without antibiotics, a first for us. It turns out being sick on a ship isn't the worst place in the world to be sick. The sea was kind to us for five whole days! Three of the five of us were laid up with fevers, coughing, headaches, sore throats, and what the doctor would confirm were respiratory infections. Thank God for cozy, quiet rooms to sleep and recover in as well as 24-hr food and drink and unlimited hot water for hot steams and showers! We were also blessed with the sweetest Filipino stateroom attendant who kept us up with fresh towels and boxes of tissue while we were quarantined away in our rooms. I ran clean out of my essential oils and puffers, lotions, and potions from my medicine bag, hoping we wouldn't need them again anyway! The healthy two of us, Clint and Carson, kept busy making new friends, playing in ping pong tournaments, watching all the shows, and learning how to rock climb!

We ventured off the ship for day trips to Muscat, Oman and Aqaba, Jordan. Both days were casual days spent wandering the towns, seeing local sights by taxi, stops for coffee and free Wi-Fi, as well as some market browsing. Both were beautiful seaside towns, rich with history and lovely Arab people. Regrettably, I wasn't dressed as conservatively as I could have been, with my knees and shoulders exposed, and it wasn't long, especially in Oman, before I felt unwanted attention in the form of glares and gawking. I was suddenly feeling disrespectful of their culture and I couldn't help but wonder what kind of a world we would live in if we choose modesty. What if we had respect for the idea that men are visual creatures? And, women are insecure enough without having to feel the need to compete with other women with breast implants parading around in string bikinis, low cut shirts, and short shorts. I don't know the answer, but I know travel leads to these kinds of questions for many, not just myself. I'm thankful for the opportunity to be prodded and challenged about my beliefs, and to be sorting through different perspectives myself.

CHAPTER 6

Oman

Royal Caribbean's Vision of the Seas was amazing! We had cruised many times before, always with Carnival, both with the kids when they were younger and without kids. Carnival is known as a less-expensive party-ship type cruise line with less glam. Royal Caribbean is perhaps a bit more sophisticated but still very family-friendly and welcoming. After a lot of roughing it over the last few months, the luxury and comfort of the ship was so much appreciated, not to mention the 24/7 availability of pizza and ice cream! The kids disappeared almost instantly, making friends at the youth club. Aside from waving occasionally across the ship when we'd spot them playing ping pong or splashing in the pool, we rarely saw them unless we arranged it ahead of time. We made it their responsibility to make it back to their room for the 1:00 am ship curfew.

I, however, got sick almost instantly. My minor flu moved quickly into my lungs and throat and my sinuses became completely plugged. At first, I was disappointed to be getting sick in this environment, but soon realized that being in one place for sixteen days (with five of them being at sea with no excursions) allowed me to just relax, eat, and sleep at my leisure without the burden of cooking meals, cleaning, and planning. It turned out to be a real blessing.

Most days I was well enough to make it up to the Lido deck for meals in the formal dining room or to sit in the sun and read while Clint buzzed off, making new friends or challenging the climbing wall. This cruise, which he felt so unsure of when we planned it, was turning into the trip highlight for all of us! I enjoyed the space and freedom after being together for months, with little to no break from each other. The kids had their own room next door to ours. Even though Rylan also got sick a few days in and spent most of his time in our bed, for the most part we had a good two weeks of badly-needed and long-overdue privacy.

Muscat, Oman was our first port before being at sea for the following 5 days. Muscat is the capital and largest city of Oman. It is an oil-rich area, and has been a vitally important trading port between the East and West since the 1st century. It is predominantly Muslim in religion and Arabic is the first language. English a close second, used by the educated and by the younger generations. We hadn't made plans for Muscat or any of the other upcoming ports except Israel. After such a busy weekend in Dubai, and with no Wi-Fi on the ship, we were officially winging it for the first time, just showing up and hoping for the best. That's how we made money mistake number two.

We shuffled off the ship after breakfast in no particular hurry as we really had nowhere to be. We decided to walk around the port and see where the wind would take us. We were immediately bombarded with physically aggressive and loud Omani tour guides shouting tour ideas and prices, some in English, some not. We refused most of them but after haggling with the most persistent one, we agreed to a city tour with stops at a bank machine for cash, a grocery store for cough drops and medicine, and short visits to the most common tourist stops. We arranged to be dropped off afterward at the souk at the entrance to the port, all for 50 Riel. This was all relayed through the English-speaking, very bossy Omani tour guide organizer to our tour guide who spoke no English. We jumped in and off we went! Our guide nodded and proceeded to point to things throughout our city tour. To what, we were never sure. Sometimes pointing meant *get out, this is an interesting view or attraction*, and sometimes pointing just meant, *look*.

Overall, the experience was unique and the city of Muscat was a beautiful ancient sea-front fortress that we thoroughly enjoyed. We focused on the fact that we were supporting an elderly tour guide who possibly had no other source of income. With no Wi-Fi for our currency app, and no idea how much Riel was in CAD dollars, we withdrew 100 Riel on a whim. We had enough to pay for the tour, and even after buying some cough drops and a stop at a local cafe for smoothies and delicious cardamom tea, we had 30 or 40 Riel to spare. It was at the cafe that we used the Wi-Fi to load our currency app to figure out how much we had spent. Our jaws hit the floor in a most painful way when we calculated that 100 Riel is actually $450 CAD. No wonder everything seemed so cheap. A quick Google search let us know that the Riel is the strongest currency in the world, and we were horrified to learn we just blew about four-days worth of budget on a tour, cough drops and tea! The leftover 40 Riel got tucked away in our wallets and we guarded it closely until we later found an exchange counter in Greece and swapped it for Euros. Lesson learned!

The other lesson I learned, to my dismay, was how *not* to dress in a conservative Muslim country. I wouldn't exactly call the knee-length walking shorts and wide-strap tank top I was wearing provocative, but upon leaving the tourist trap areas and venturing into local grocery stores and banks, we were reminded that men in these countries don't typically see exposed limbs and snug-fitting shirts. I'm not exactly small chested, either. I felt like a complete floozy and terrible for exposing myself on their territory. I was gawked at, whistled at, and I wanted to apologize to every wife I encountered. I wasn't longing for a Canadian winter parka, but at a minimum, I should have thrown a shawl over my shoulders and considered wearing light pants. It was a 2 km walk back to the ship from the souk and as usual, I took up the lonely rear, with Clint at least a block ahead of me. Every man that walked by would stop and stare at my legs. As if they weren't obvious enough coming toward me; I could feel them following me with their eyes from behind. I felt terrible and couldn't get back on that ship fast enough.

Returning from our day ashore, I felt worse than ever: exhausted, stuffed up, and coughing non stop. We all looked forward to dinner and a nap. Thank God, we now had 5 glorious days at sea to soak up the sun, eat and drink at our leisure, relax and get better. Next stop: Aqaba, Jordan.

> **Travel Tip - Research the Omani currency well and know what things will cost in your local currency.**

CHAPTER 7

At Sea

We've been on 5 cruises over the years and most people know that the sea can be a moody beast. You honestly never know what you are going to get. These 5 days were a *dream*. The sea was calm, smooth, and gorgeous. We sailed through the Red Sea making our way to the Suez Canal with barely a wave and with the full sun shining in blue skies. The movie Captain Phillips was filmed in these same waters. It was based on the true story of a captain of a cargo ship who was held hostage by North African pirates, higher than a kite on cheap drugs, who wanted his money and goods. As it turns out, this is a normal kind of occurrence on the Red Sea, so when a ship as grand and lavish as The Vision of the Seas sails through, they need to take precautions. This meant armed guards and an expert security company to patrol the waters to keep the 3000 ship guests safe. We also had 'dark nights,' meaning that for three nights through the most dangerous area, room lights had to be off for those in an ocean-view or outside rooms, and all outside public areas were closed and darkened from sunset on. Guards with night vision goggles were scattered among the ship on high alert throughout the night. The kids were entertained by their presence. They told us that they, with a group of their friends, stopped a guard and asked to see through his sniper scope— which he obliged. It was quite the experience! We made it through with nothing to report and ship life returned to normal by the fourth night. I was especially relieved because a couple of months prior to departure, I had received an email notifying us of this dangerous passage through the Red Sea. I knew about the dark nights but was too scared to tell Clint as he was already hesitant about the cruise because of the cost. The last thing I needed was for him to freak out and want to cancel. I decided to keep it to myself and pray for the best. Everything turned out fine!

Rylan's flu took a turn for the worse on the 3rd day at sea. His fever increased, his cough worsened, and he was lethargic and would not eat anything. I had been pumping all of us so full of essential oils, honey and tea, grapefruit seed extract (my tried and true faithful immune support) and anything else I could get my hands on. I did my best to keep him hydrated and made him take cold showers to try to get his fever down, but after a few days I had to get him to a ship doctor. I just couldn't take his fever anymore. So, for a budget-breaking $300 CAD, he was looked over and it was confirmed that, thank God, he didn't have pneumonia and with some Tylenol he would likely bounce back within a day or two. And he did! He lost a few days in youth club and hanging with his new friends, but before long he was back at it. I hadn't gotten any worse, but I was definitely not getting better either and our next port, which I did not have the energy for, was fast approaching.

Clint and I met a lovely young couple from Australia at lunch one day at sea, who would become our ship buddies for the rest of the cruise. Ty and Melissa were a new couple, and on their own adventure of a lifetime, travelling on a 6-month journey similar to ours. They had been to India, Sri Lanka, and Southeast Asia, and would be heading to Europe next and then North America. They became great friends to us and we still stay in touch online. I spent many nights in the steam room on the ship, nursing my cold and chatting good old-fashioned girl talk with Melissa, comparing travel notes and talking about our futures, while Clint and Ty met for snacks, ping pong games, and competing on the climbing wall. It was lovely and refreshing to have girl time. We shared an instant friendship and never ran out of things to do or talk about. We took in a lovely interdenominational Good Friday service in the ship theatre and continued to enjoy 5-star evening meals while the boys gorged on pizza and buffet to their heart's content.

"All *free!*" they would constantly remark.

To which I would reply, "Not free, just prepaid!"

The cruise brought us over five months into our journey and by then we were maybe, *just a little,* starting to miss our peeps and home. Braden was constantly commenting on missing his bed and room, Rylan missed random things, and Carson was still Carson, with a slight improvement in attitude as of late. Clint was doing fine, still not missing anything and loving every minute! My anxiety had taken a back seat as we were settled and comfortable. Besides still being sick, I was doing great mentally and thoroughly enjoyed myself and all of the family time we had on our days at sea. Travel had become our new normal.

Travel Tip - For cruises, I always scour the cruise line's website for floor plans and find a room below where we will spend most of our time (the lido deck, the kids club and the pools). We don't mind the jaunt to the other end for formal dinner and shows once every evening but during the day it is so nice to just run up and down, sometimes only one flight of stairs to be where all of our action is! Also-avoid rooms bordering an elevator shaft, the foot traffic can go late into the night and be incredibly noisy.

CHAPTER 8

Jordan

We sailed into Aqaba, Jordan on Monday morning, April 16th. Clint and Carson were pumped and ready to hit the streets, adventuring wherever the wind took them! After a week at sea, let's be real, Carson was on the hunt for Wi-Fi. The other two boys were cranky and not wanting to disembark. Melissa and Ty were spending the day apart as he had booked a group tour out to Wadi Rum and Petra and she couldn't afford it, so she had talked about joining us wherever we were planning on going, which was totally fine until now. I was still so, so sick. To my miserable sadness and dismay, I just couldn't get the energy to get myself up. I felt bad leaving Melissa to awkwardly join Clint and Carson alone, but she insisted it was fine, and Clint, being the social butterfly that he is, was fine with it too. So off they went without us, while I cried and spent the morning in bed sick and devastated. The other kids went off with their friends, happy to not have to leave the ship. By noon, I woke up somewhat refreshed, tracked the kids down, ate some lunch, and made the decision that we were getting off! We would be ported until about 5:00 pm so we still had lots of time and I personally wanted a quick Wi-Fi Facebook check-in with friends and family to let them know we were still alive. So off we went to Aqaba, Jordan, hoping to find the other half of our family too!

We bussed into town, wandered aimlessly around and stopped off near a McDonald's where we unsuccessfully tried to hotspot. Next, we tried the coffee shop next door. They boasted free Wi-Fi, so we took an outside table in the sun, ordered sodas and hummus with chips and tomatoes and hopped on their Wi-Fi to let everyone know that we were safe and sound and still having fun! Not 10 minutes into our little outing did Clint and the gang stroll by our coffee shop, as they too were looking for a quick bite and some Wi-Fi. We reunited, shared some Middle Eastern treats and got caught up on their day. They filled us in that they had mostly just explored by foot, taking in the sights and architecture. We paid the bill and then shopped for our signature fridge magnet souvenir that we had collected in every country we had stopped in since we left, and made our way back to the ship for dinner.

Dinner was always a fun time to reunite with friends that we had made on the ship, and exchange stories of adventures in port. Ty had had a fabulous time at Petra, but when he ran into a few other cruise mates along the way he learned that they hadn't splurged on the expensive ship excursion but simply paid a local taxi driver to take them out and back, and they had had just as great a time. Clint was regretful that he hadn't researched Jordan whatsoever after discovering what a historical gem Petra was in world and biblical history. He was even more disappointed to have missed out knowing that he and Carson could have done it very inexpensively. The photos were breathtaking and the experience would have quite likely been a trip highlight. Another lesson learned. Overall, our time in Jordan was short and sweet but memorable. We had two more days at sea and our upcoming port in Israel was approaching quickly. I felt the pressure more than ever to hurry up and feel better. We had booked big group tours there and had spent a large budget to see it. For me, being down and out was not an option! Time would tell.

Travel Tip - Don't waste money on expensive ship tours. Trust the locals and see the area on your own and do NOT skip on Petra. Huge regret of ours.

Blog Post: April 2017

I'm not exactly sure what I expected, nor can I remember what notions I had about The Holy Land prior to visiting, First off, we were not in Israel for long enough to have anything near a complete experience. Three of us were still sick, hacking, and sniffling, and a 5:45 am wakeup call is never good after several sleepless nights. We had also chosen to do Jerusalem independently instead of with a group tour to save $300 CAD. It may or may not have been worth it, the verdict is still out. Our day involved a shuttle ride to Ashdod City Centre Mall, which arrived too late to connect to our city bus to Jerusalem, which in turn caused us to miss the free walking tour that we had planned for 11:00 am. We took the time instead to enjoy free McDonald's Wi-Fi, hoping that some wandering around Jerusalem Old City and our second tour, scheduled for 2:00 pm would suffice.

After an hour-long bus ride and yet another taxi to the Old City, we found ourselves smack dab in the middle of the busiest, craziest, mayhem. It was Holy Week, otherwise known as Passover. Traffic was backed up for blocks and there were people everywhere including police and soldiers.

It was also Easter, which I was hoping the hoopla was for. Easter is for Christians though, and Christians are not easy to find in Jerusalem. Instead, there were a fascinating mix of Jews: Orthodox Jews, traditional Jews, secular Jews, practicing and non-practicing Jews, and all of the Jews had come to The Old City to celebrate Passover. Most had huge families of at least four kids, but usually up to six or seven kids. There were also Muslims about and plenty of tourists! So we wandered around aimlessly, regretting having missed our first tour and cramming what we could into one short hour before our next tour of the Mount of Olives began.

The weather and moderate temperature of the day couldn't have been better for a three-hour walking tour of the Mount of Olives. Our guide was a lovely young Jewish man from Tel Aviv who took us through the local churches and monuments on the Mount of Olives, which turns out is important to all three major religions! We saw the spot where they believe Jesus ascended to Heaven after his death and resurrection, and where he appeared to several people over the following forty days. Unfortunately, it is now a Muslim mosque and is only used as a church twice each year (for our Christian Christmas and Easter.)

We also walked through beautiful overlooks of Jerusalem city as well as the most important Jewish cemetery in the world. The Jews believe this to be the site where the Messiah, once he comes, will arrive, and that the dead will rise from those graves. We visited the Garden of Gethsemane and the Church of Nations, which contains the rock that they believe Jesus wept on prior to being betrayed by Judas and denied by Peter. We also saw the cave where it is believed that Jesus taught the Lord's Prayer to his disciples. Our day ended on a bit of a sour note as we faced a long jaunt back up the hill to the Old City, spent almost two frantic hours trying to catch a taxi. We had to race through the bus terminal in order to catch the last bus back to our port, not to mention that the shuttle back to the ship took forever to come! We finally made it back onto the ship at 9:35 pm, just as it was preparing to leave port at 10:00 pm. Too close a call for my comfort!. The delays and close call are the reason we question whether the independent tour was the right idea, but we made it, and that's all the counts!

We had an early start the next day in Haifa. We boarded a van for an organized Biblical Tour of Galilee, which went quite a bit better than the previous day had, thank God! After visiting a beautiful lookout over the Bahai Gardens, we drove an hour out to the Sea of Galilee and listened to some of the most interesting Jesus stories told by another local Jewish tour guide. With enthusiasm and passion he explained to us Jesus' childhood in Capernaum; showed us the hill overlooking the area where he delivered The Sermon on the Mount; the Jordan River where he had been baptized by John the Baptist; and the place where he blessed Peter and gave him the mission to continue to build the church. Both days were eye opening, shocking, interesting, and very confusing. I had come with an expectation to feel closer to God, walking where Jesus walked, and witnessing his legacy. I thought I would sense his presence by being present where he once had been, but I didn't. None of us did. Instead, I felt overwhelmed by the complete management of all of the monuments by the Catholic Church. The burning incense, the hanging rosary beads, the lanterns, the altars, and priests bowing and kissing the floor where they believed Mary was buried: It was just way too foreign and too religious for our taste. Not to mention the blaring of the Muslim call to prayer that goes out over loud speakers throughout the entire city five times each day, another disconnect for us. I also was confused by these Jewish tour guides who spend their life and make a living believing and teaching that Jesus was who he claimed to be, rose from the dead, performed many miracles, and essentially changed the world. When pressed, they would say, 'I'm a Jew and I can't believe he was the Messiah, I have to disregard it.'

I'm left knowing and trusting that God is in full control. He knows everything from the beginning to the end, including his plan for the Jews, the Muslims, and us Christians. In the meantime, I feel extremely challenged to study and am ultimately intrigued by how Jesus has changed history and the world, is known to be alive and well by people worldwide, but in this small unique country, his birthplace where it all began, he's not worshipped. Where I expected him to be everywhere, he felt almost nowhere; a mystery. Clint is determined to come back, but I am on the fence! Being a small part of the massive worship gatherings of believers at Hillsong Church in Australia, and worshipping together with Thai believers in Thailand, both did more to encourage my faith than any day in Israel did. Each to his own; that's the beauty of the Christian faith!

CHAPTER 9

Israel

Part One

We spent two more relaxing days at sea without incident. We took in the great shows at night. I read tonnes of books and continued to take advantage of the glorious steam room after hitting the walking track every day, even though I was still stuffed up and hacking. Back in Australia, we had stopped in at a tourist information booth (as we always did). While chatting with a volunteer there, I found out that she had previously gone on the exact cruise we were booked to go on. While giving us some tips she suddenly remembered that they had been given a free Future Israel tour as compensation for something that had gone wrong on their cruise. They had no plan to ever use it, so she forwarded it along to my email address in case we wanted to take the tour. I researched tour guides and poured over travel blogs and Trip Advisor for days until we finally conceded that there was no cheap way to get a good visit to Jerusalem and Haifa, Israel. But, we were determined to do it as best we could on the cheap, and the free tour coupon helped. For $500 CAD, I booked all five of us for a Christian-oriented five-hour tour, departing from Haifa Israel, that would cover the majestic Bahai Gardens, Nazareth, Capernaum, the Jordan River, and the Sea of Galilee. But that was Haifa.

First we had to sort out how we wanted to spend our day in Jerusalem. Our port, Ashdod, Israel was actually an hour's drive out of Jerusalem. I roughly pieced together a plan to take a shuttle to a mall, then a bus to Jerusalem city centre, then a taxi to Old Jerusalem where we could take a free (donation only) walking tour. We would follow that up with lunch and another inexpensive walking tour of the Garden of Gethsemane, Church of the Nazarene, and a couple of other sites. It seemed that we would have plenty of time left over to backtrack those steps to get back to our ship by dinner time!

It started off well and we hit the mall, where we took over their Wi-Fi yet again. Carson was deeply distracted by his phone messages, acting frantic and not wanting to go anywhere. We thought he was just being bratty, but found out later that he was dealing with some news from home privately. I went looking for a bathroom which didn't go well. The doors of the only woman's restroom I could find had been closed and locked for cleaning. I paced and waited impatiently outside which took forty-five minutes, which made us miss the first bus, which we knew would lead to us missing our first walking tour. Clint was not happy, but I was moody and determined to *not* climb onto a bus for an hour-long ride until I had used the washroom. We made the next bus and made sure to take in all the sights and scenery that we could as we made our way through the countryside and small villages to Jerusalem. It had a remarkably North American feeling, with nice highways, signage in English as well as Hebrew, modern looking people, and beautiful cars. It was only the ancient, cobblestone, adobe-style villages dotting the surrounding hillsides that reminded us where we actually were, and that Israel is a place rich with history.

Our bus took us straight to the centre of Old Jerusalem, which was hidden behind a high rock wall up on a hill overlooking the valley. We passed hordes of large Orthodox Jewish families that were piled into busses and heading in the same direction that we were. They were going to pray and commemorate Passover, as our visit occurred during Holy Week. The Orthodox Jewish families looked exactly as they do in the movies, with numerous children and the men in top hats with long ringleted peyot, scruffy beards, and white collared shirts with suspenders or coat jackets. Orthodox Jews are very devout and are the majority in Jerusalem (their birth place), and they were pouring into the Old City during Holy Week by the thousands. We were lucky or unlucky to be there then, depending on who you talk to. It felt special to us and we found ourselves observing, just taking it all in. Since we had sadly missed our morning with Sandman's Walking Tours, we now had time to wander freely, find some lunch, and stroll Old Jerusalem's cobblestone streets. We explored food stalls, trinket stores, and old church alleyways.

By 1:00 pm it was time to meet for our afternoon walking tour, which was hosted by Matt, a lovely young local man from Tel Aviv. We piled into Matt's van and he drove to our first destination, from where we would walk for the rest of the tour. Plan A was to catch a taxi back to the bus after the tour, which would take us back to the mall, where we would catch the shuttle back to the ship. It was risky—cruise ships don't wait for anyone— but I felt optimistic. For the entire trip I was the chief organizer, researcher, and the one who booked and coordinated everything. When things went amazing it was on me, but when things went south, that was on me too. No one else, including Clint, ever really knew what we were doing until we were doing it, nor did they care. This is usually fine, except whenever things didn't go as planned, then I carried the burden of everyone's stress, which I don't handle well.

Back to being hopeful: the tour kicked off at the Mount of Olives. Matt was a local but not Jewish. He knew his stuff and was knowledgeable about the area's history. He didn't skimp on the Jesus details but it was here that I started to pick up on the fact that he had no problem speaking of Jesus as someone special and world changing, but that it didn't matter to him personally. He spoke with profound and genuine excitement about Jesus's miracles, reminding us about the prophecies spoken about Christ eons before his coming, and about how his life affected the area and eventually, the world. But for Matt it ended there, which was very difficult for me to understand. For a Christian like me, that's just when things got exciting. The birthplace of our faith was behind those walls and in those hills, and the world was never the same after Jesus showed up, so to seemingly dismiss it all was beyond confusing. He was careful to specify 'reportedly' when leading us through different sites and remnants which I guess he was obligated to do as no one present for those events is actually here to confirm nor deny the 'reports.' Overall it was educational and exciting to experience first hand. Matt led us through the Garden of Gethsemane where Peter was told he would deny Jesus and where Jesus fasted and prayed and awaited his arrest. We explored the Church of Ascension, where it's believed he ascended into heaven after his resurrection, as well as the 'grotto' remnants of where they believe he wrote and taught the disciples The Lord's Prayer. The word grotto was used as that was the best description for it. Picture an ancient rock cave as you descend down into it from a carved-out stone staircase. The Church of Disciples, as it's known today, contains wall-sized slates of marble, all adorned with The Lord's Prayer in dozens of languages. It was a work of art, spectacular to behold. I bought a souvenir here for my bestie who was currently in Haiti. It was a smaller, book-sized printout of the prayer in Creole. It was inexpensive, easy to carry, and I couldn't resist. I wish I'd have bought an English one for myself. We were toured through the church where it is believed Jesus' mother Mary died. It was now a Catholic church and was drowned out with incense, rosary beads hanging from the ceilings, and small groups of people who were scattered about, chanting. I suppose they could have been praying, but I'm not Catholic and do not relate to their rituals so this was just another memorial with little meaning for us.

By this point in the tour it was impossible to miss the Muslim influence dominating the city, whether it was the gigantic mosque taking up half of the skyline, the drawl of the Muslim call to prayer over loudspeakers five times each day, or the Muslim ownership of several of the Christian churches and memorials that we visited. It was noteworthy to me that in the geographic birthplace of our faith, not much of our faith remained. The place *felt* very religious but didn't deliver the spiritual connection we had hoped to find, at all. I have since been told that if we had taken Christian tours from a Christian perspective and had more time to take in the sights and sounds of the countryside and surrounding areas, we might have felt differently. Who is to know? We had what we had and overall it was memorable.

Matt bade us farewell and informed us that taxis were just a block away and that we shouldn't have trouble securing a ride back to the bus. We stopped at a little snack bar to grab some chips and soda and began our trek to track down a taxi. Braden did a quick check of the surroundings as usual, and noticed that Clint had left his phone behind yet again. This time he left it at the bar counter, almost half a block behind us by the time

Braden realized. We snatched it up and vowed to keep quiet until Clint noticed it missing; maybe a little longer depending on his stress level when he realized.

Our Plan A to return to the ship got off to a rough start as we wandered aimlessly looking for a non-existent taxi. We called a few times to order one, but none ever showed. We decided to walk up the long steep hill back towards the Old City, which was the direction we needed to go, hoping that someone would notice and take mercy on us. By now we were hot, hungry and out of water again. We were *always* out of water. We stopped and asked some armed guards, who were guarding nothing as far as we could tell, how far we should go to find a taxi. They just pointed up the hill, so we carried on. I was exhausted and the hill was killing my sick lungs. Our stress levels rose by the minute as time was *seriously* ticking. We didn't even know what time the last bus would leave for the mall, nor the last shuttle for the ship. I may have cried at this point and cursed my entire crappy plan. We should have just bucked up for a real tour that would have guaranteed us a punctual return to the ship. An hour or more passed with many failed taxi hailings, when finally our Israeli taxi angel agreed to squeeze all of us into his car although we were one passenger over limit. We had to promise to keep Rylan down and out of sight. So Rylan hit the floor and never got another glance of Jerusalem, just the sight and smell of dirty, stinky feet.

About ten minutes into our twenty-five minute drive to the bus station, Clint began the 'pat down.' That's what we've named his familiar gestures that signal to us that he's lost his phone or wallet, patting himself down and searching every pocket for his missing item. The kids all looked at me with big eyes, asking silently, *do we tell him we have it?*

"What 'cha lookin' for?" I casually asked him.

"I can't find my phone," he replied. He also remembered that his ship ID and room card—necessary to reboard the ship—are stashed in the back of the phone, which proposed another sticky situation.

"Think back—when did you last use it?" I coached him, adding, "Should we go back and find it?"

Braden was beyond worried by this time and clearly wanting to tell Clint we had the phone. But, nope. I'd had a rough afternoon and needed a laugh, frankly. And I thought Clint could use a lesson in keeping track of his stuff. I was determined to teach it to him.

Clint started doing what he always does, downplaying reality and persuading himself—and attempting to convince us—that everything would be fine and that it was a crappy old phone anyway. Never mind the fact that we'd have to pay hundreds of dollars to replace it with a new one, and that the new one would likely be useless once we got home. His lack of concern took all the fun out of it for me. If he was stressed, he was definitely not showing it.

We reached the bus station with half an hour to spare based on the departure times we found on a sign. We used the washrooms, grabbed food and water, and waited for the last bus of the day to our port, Ashdod. While we waited, Braden decided he couldn't take it anymore and pulled out the phone. He started to play phone games on it, waiting to see how long it would take for Clint to notice it was his. It took about fifteen minutes, and the look of relief on Clint's face was completely worth it. The rest of us enjoyed a hearty laugh while he tried not to be annoyed.

Our bus arrived right on time and got us back to Ashdod mall with another half hour to spare before the last shuttle of the evening to the ship. I used the time to buy even more cough medicine and throat drops, hoping to take the edge off my horrible cough and sinus congestion while we shuttled back. We made it right in time for evening dinner and drinks, and our favourite time of the day when we got to reunite with our ship friends and compare the day's journeys. We traded stories and shared experiences. My stress dissolved, and all was well in the world. Tomorrow would be a new day and I couldn't help but wonder what else Israel had in store for us.

Israel Part Two

We joined about twelve other ship guests at a pre-arranged meeting spot for our grand tour of Haifa, Israel around 9:00 am. I chose this tour because we were gifted a free pass for one person, emailed to us by some new friends in Australia, but even so, the cost came in at a hefty $500 CAD. After our stressful day in Jerusalem the day before, I had high hopes that this tour would be impressive and easier on my mental state. I relaxed right off the bat, knowing our return time to the ship at the end of the day was guaranteed.

Our first stop was the Bahai Temple and Gardens which is the main holy site for the Baha'i faith worldwide. It was absolutely gorgeous and meticulously well-maintained. We learned that the Baha'i Faith was born many miles away in Persia (Iran), but after the founder Bahaullah was banished from home many times, he exiled here in Israel at the end of his life and had been buried in the vicinity. The Baha'i adhere to the cardinal teaching of their faith, which is to seek to create unity based on the principle of oneness with humanity. They continue to abide by the faith's law that members must obey the laws of the land where they live and not participate in partisan politics. The Bahai World Centre brings in 700 volunteer staff from around the world and is a symbol of the unity of humanity. It provides an example of how people of many diverse national and religious backgrounds can come together in harmony and work for the peace and prosperity of the world. It was lovely and serene and interesting but we were here to see and hear about Jesus!

We took a beautiful scenic drive through the Israeli countryside en route to Capernaum, passing by turn-offs to places such as Nazareth and Bethlehem. That made me wish hard that we had more time. That's the thing with cruises, they are great for getting a taste of a place. If you don't love it, check it off the list and be glad you only had a day. But when you love a place, it feels rushed and you yearn to stay longer. I had anticipated this, knowing how rich in history Israel is, but I knew I had no time for regrets. We had to make the most of the time allotted. We passed by the Mount of Beatitudes where Jesus miraculously fed 3,000 people, and listened to stories of how Jesus fled to the countryside as he was healing and performing miracles because the authorities were starting to question him with hostility. He traveled the area by foot, teaching and preaching and changing the world. We took one of my favourite family photos of the five of us in front of The Sea of Galilee, which looked more like a large glass lake. We got another amazing photo in front of the ruins of the church where Jesus was believed to have taught his last sermon. We wandered through several other ruins, took in our tour guide's captivating stories, and found ourselves in complete awe of it all. Had Jesus really preached here? Had He commanded the attention of the crowd He spoke to the same way our tour guide did with us? Did they believe Him? Were they skeptical? Obviously the Bible answers these questions and more, but there was something magical about being there, the birthplace of it all, and resting in it. I silently prayed and thanked God for fulfilling His promises and sending Jesus, just as He said He would for thousands of years prior.

I reflected on how the world was never the same after He came. His message had spread like wildfire back then, by word of mouth throughout the Promised Land, but also beyond the walls of Jerusalem and out into the world. No one before or since has had the impact Jesus did on society. Our calendars are even designed around him being here, with his life marking the division of history between BC and AD! I thought about the miracles He performed and the privilege those people had of witnessing such major historical events. Events that would endure through time to become stories to us, so many years later. Could they have known that they would always be a part of history?

Our tour guide described himself as a secular Jew. Even after enthusiastically describing how Jesus impacted the area and changed the future of the world forever, when we pressed him about it, he still believed that Jesus wasn't the Messiah that the Jews are still waiting for. Over thousands of years, 200 prophecies have been fulfilled, many miraculous signs and wonders have been performed, and it's still not enough? This was perplexing to the Christians in our group. *What does the Messiah have left to do?* We all wondered aloud. *What else is there?* He told us in so many words that he believes it all happened but chooses to disregard it. It was an interesting perspective to say the least.

From there we boarded the bus and headed to the Jordan River, but not before stopping for an amazing lunch of souvlaki, rice, and pitas under a tent in the desert. We arrived at the Jordan River tourist information stop under the mid-afternoon sun. The Jordan River is a significant place to behold for the Christian faith. Jesus was baptized there and it is known that John the Baptist performed many, if not all, of his baptisms there as well, not necessarily at the exact location of this tourist trap, but somewhere along the river.

We were greeted with this sign at the entrance:

**In those days Jesus came from
Nazareth of Galilee and was
baptized by John in the Jordan.
And when he came up out of
the water, immediately he saw the
heavens opened and the Spirit
descending upon him like a dove,
and a voice came from heaven;
"Thou art my beloved Son; with
thee I am well pleased."
Mark 1:9-11**

This scripture says it all. People and church groups come from all around the world to be baptized here, some for a second time, just for the experience alone. It was a beautiful, highly memorable part of our journey and I am so grateful that we were able to partake of it. We wandered the boardwalks that bordered the river banks and followed the river a short walk down and back. We bought our Israel magnet and hopped back on the bus for our quiet return journey to the ship. Israel was fresh in our minds and I knew that it would sit with us for a long time, and perhaps change us in unknown ways. The tour had *definitely* been worth it.

Travel Tip - Use TripAdvisor! They were so handy for every single detail in Israel, the forum especially. I asked about bus numbers and mall names and tour guide leads. I always received a speedy personal reply from someone. It saved the day for planning.

We've been on the road for over five months now. We likely have around three to go but we're still unsure as we refuse to talk about ending the trip, nor do we have any idea how to wrap it up. People from home and that we meet along the way keep asking, and we continually give the same answers. We don't know, and we still don't really care. I would be lying though, if I didn't admit to feeling slightly anxious lately when I think about it.

Carson hasn't really ever come around. He has moments where he seems ok (usually when he's found Wi-Fi) and he is generally amicable, but overall, he clearly still does not want to be along for the trip. We don't talk about it as it guarantees an argument which rarely ends well or has any positive outcome. Usually, he just presses to know when we'll be home, which, again, we don't know. So he keeps to himself and doesn't seem to enjoy anything, but doesn't really complain either. His sulking hasn't had enough power to ruin it for the rest of us, but he has made it difficult, at times, to enjoy our adventure. I find this deeply disappointing and heartbreaking to be honest, as I had such high hopes. This wasn't the dream for me. He is still very much a teen, moody and lethargic, forgetting everything everywhere, and sleeping long hours. Ironically, he is a fantastic traveller. He is adventurous with food, can walk for hours at a time without complaining, likes to keep busy, can convert almost any currency in his head in a heartbeat, and nothing seems to stress him out. He is very low-maintenance in that regard, which takes the edge off my frustration, and I do try to acknowledge his cooperation. We still share a good line of communication and if I ask him, he'll talk to me, so that's good. We've had wonderful conversations about our time in Israel and he was overall impressed with The Middle East, Dubai in particular.

Braden has been a life saver! That child has recovered so many items that we've left behind: phones, water bottles, hoodies. He knows where everything is all the time, notices everything and everyone, and is the best at keeping track of our location and knowing how to get back to our accommodations! He reads signs and maps, understands directions, and is constantly re-routing us to our destination. His childhood policeman skills have saved our butts many times! It took him a while to prove himself—what grown father wants to be constantly told by his thirteen year old that we are heading to the WRONG terminal at the airport AGAIN, or that we took the wrong turn to the hotel AGAIN—but after he proved us wrong a handful of times, we started to listen. He is almost always right! He is generally a good sport, has a best friend for life in his little brother, and has also adapted well to travel. He continues to share with me everything that he thinks and feels, which can be exhausting, but it's what he needs so I listen the best I can. His sensitivity comes with quite a bit of drama and emotion, too much blaming sometimes, and less accountability than I'd like to see. Overall, he is wise and has amazing common sense, so we work with him through these growing pains and the victim mentality that he tends to have. He misses the comfort of home more than the rest of us, He misses his best friends, having a pet, privacy, and routine. He works tirelessly editing and creating things for the kids' vlog and is completely self taught. Every time he creates something I am still shocked at how much he's learned on his own, with crappy equipment and software, and barely any internet access.

Rylan has changed the most by far. He has found his voice somewhere along the way, and uses it loud and clear, no longer afraid to share his feisty point of view. He has learned to pay attention to detail. He is now able to keep track of where we are, what turns we need to take, and how to read a map. I'm sure in one way or another he will always live in some sort of oblivion, but overall he is learning to tune in to his surroundings. He's still a sleepyhead and can never get enough cuddles, but we've barely seen him on the cruise, so maybe that's changed too! He's generally a good sport, but hates walking and is not usually into the same things we are. He likes the glitz and glam of travel, the waterslides, arcades, and theme parks, but has no use for history, or museums or any tours that involve walking or hiking. This is likely typical for twelve year olds, but is annoying nonetheless. He's still a choosy eater, preferring to snack all day and neglect meals. He is by far the least accommodating when it comes to eating, and it's hard to keep his constant snack needs satisfied. The cruise has been a dream for dealing with that; a very welcome sixteen-day break for me.

Clint was born to travel. That guy is in the zone! I can't say it enough, he is a trooper: always positive, open to adventure, still frugal, never sick (except for a constant returning headache and sore back), loves new foods, loves meeting new people, needs less sleep than the rest of us, and adapts to everything well. He has learned to read and relax but can be on the go all day if needed. He does not want to go home. He misses people more than I do, but that comes as no surprise.. We have had some major bumps in learning to be together 24/7. We'd had a hard time being together at home most times, before we even left. For years, it's been me and kids, so to suddenly have him around all the time being bossy and trying to fix things that don't need fixing, and constantly reminding us what we can't afford took a few months to work through, but he's found his groove. We've had to learn to communicate through managing money, driving, boredom, exhaustion, language barriers, and currency conversion. Basically, life on the road is the same as it is at home. You take your issues with you. Travel makes some things harder and some easier. And there is never any privacy so we argue in public and in front of the kids, which got old really quick for everyone. Just another thing we had to adjust to. I'm sure he will settle back into a routine quickly when we get back home, but for now, he's in travel mode and doesn't want to think about going back.

I'm all over the place. I'm generally a recluse, quite happy to be alone, to read or write in my room away from people and crowds. I thought being on the road would bring me back to my previous, less stressed-out self, that Shauna who enjoyed being social. But as of yet... nope. I fluctuate between loving the freedom of travel, appreciating time with my family, and enjoying new experiences, to being withdrawn, feeling down, needing quiet, missing my space, and feeling worried, anxious, and generally not having fun. It comes and goes like a wave. I hate feeling inconsistent and I don't trust my feelings so I don't try to change them. This doesn't mean, by the way, that in moments of struggle I want to go home. I just struggle with where I'm at on any given day. I suspect my hormonal health is the root of it and there is nothing I can do about it right now. So, in the meantime I cope.

Our plans for the next 3 months are minimal which grieves my planning nature. The cash flow isn't aligning with the remaining timeline either, so again, I'm left trying to balance planning with not planning and trying to go with the flow which is not easy. Intellectually, I know that I will look back and see how this trip shaped and changed us. We will miss things and want to go back to some places, but right now, when it's hard it's hard. I'd love to have more control over my emotions, but in reality I don't.

The cruise has been, without a doubt, a highlight for us all. The relaxation, food, entertainment and new friends, not to mention the countries we've visited, have been just an amazing experience, even with having been sick. It's been sixteen days in one spot without having to pack up and move, which is a record for our five months travelling so far. The last record was fifteen days. We don't count Australia, where we were static for three months, but constantly on the road. We've had such a great time on the cruise and are not ready to leave, but new adventures await!

Europe and the UK (and the cold, which we are not prepared for) are just around the corner, and we are looking forward to that! The boys are blowing out of all of their clothes. We're down a hoodie and a couple of shoes, and their pants all look like knickers! I'm hoping we can make it with what we have over the next few weeks until Mexico.

In the meantime, we learn new things about each other every day, we grow and we struggle, we argue and we get tired, but we are having the time of our lives overall. Travel is awesome and life changing. I think it is a must do for any family! Life is good, and God is awesome.

CHAPTER 10

Greece

We ported in sunny and ancient Athens bright and early in the morning on Sunday April 16th, 2017 and were finally able to exchange the 40 Riel that had been burning a hole in our pocket since Oman. We collected about 100 Euro, put it into safe keeping for the rest of our time in Europe, and went on to search for something exciting to do since we hadn't made specific plans for our time in Greece.

We headed for the lineup of Big Bus Tours parked right outside the ship. The lineup was small, and there were a few tours to choose from, but we just grabbed the first one heading into town that offered a great price for a family of five. Traveling with a family our size can be an absolute nightmare. Getting taxis almost always means a more expensive van or SUV, or that one of us had to go without a seatbelt. Riding without seatbelts was common in third world countries, but once we landed in more developed nations with stricter laws, it was always a mandatory taxi or Uber upgrade.

Hotel rooms in North America have always been somewhat of a pain for our family of five as well. When the boys were little, I only ever booked one room and hauled a fold-out foamie with us if the hotel didn't offer free cots. We became skilled at dropping off half of us at the front of the hotel, and then shuffling the rest of us in through the back. We did this successfully for years. That strategy was literally impossible on the front half of this trip as we couldn't haul a foamie or extra bedding around with us. And, the boys were much larger now so it just wasn't feasible to expect them to sleep on pillows on the floor anymore, or squeeze onto a tiny couch like they used to. Earlier in the trip, my bookings always started by searching for what rooms were available for five people, then comparing those options to what was available for four to see if I could save extra person charges if we'd all sleep comfortably. Often I'd have to switch back to five and pay for a larger or adjoining room, which is never cheap. Once we reached Europe it was *impossible* to not have to book two rooms, minimum. Most hotels and Airbnb's had a two-person maximum so it took some clever research and planning to find anything we could all fit into on a budget.

We climbed the winding staircase of the double-decker bus to reach the top, open-air section and grabbed seats. The driver had distributed earbuds for our audio tour and Greek music was blaring in the background, adding beautifully to the ambiance as we made our way along the Greek seaside into Athens with the wind blowing through our hair. We passed open-air markets and bakeries, restaurants putting their sandwich boards out for the day, and shops just beginning to open up. This was a hop-on hop-off bus tour, so the plan was to head first to the Acropolis and then wander from there. Unfortunately, being that it was Easter Sunday, the Acropolis, other ruins, and most every major tourist attraction was closed but we were still able to wander around. (I made sure later to get my 'Happy Easter Sunday from Athens, Greece' selfie for Facebook.) We met up with Ty and Melissa, who were also bummed to not be able to tour the Acropolis, and continued on together with them for the rest of our day in port.

We took a memorable photo in front of the Panathenaic Arena. The boys were thrilled to be able to climb the ancient rocks and pillars of every cool place we stopped at. Ancient Greece was turning out to be rock-climbing heaven! We ventured into central Athens as lunch time approached. The bakery windows were lavish with rows of sweets and treats that were unidentifiable to us but reasonably priced. I had so much trouble trying to choose just one! We settled on divine meat pastries with a salad and soup, and I snapped up a stash of sweets to dive into later. Athens is just remarkable, and quickly became one of my and Clint's favourite ports—somewhere we'd like to come back to. Maybe not Athens per se, but Greece for sure. A one-day stop could never do it justice. We continued to tour through the city core by bus, grabbing at branches with oranges hanging overhead as we cruised by, admiring wall after wall of graffiti that adorned the cityscape, and happened to notice (first by the smell) a full lamb being roasted out on a makeshift patio rotisserie.

We stayed on the bus for the longer tour that wound out along the coastline and beaches, rather than get off and head back to the ship. It was still mid afternoon and dinner wouldn't be served until 6:00 pm. It was a long, quiet, ride spent mostly watching beach-goers and soaking in the views and sunshine. We all hopped off once for some unique ocean photos and then made our way back to The Vision of the Seas for a nap and dinner. Athens gave us another great day in port, and had been my favourite place visited during the trip to date! I vowed to return one day.

Travel Tip - If you have monkeys for children, Greece (Athens) was a free rock climbing parkour paradise!

Blog Post: April 2017

We woke up in Venice, Italy to a cold and windy day, with no coffee waiting, no one making our beds, no friends waiting for the kids, no ping pong... Oh right! The cruise was over. It had been a fantastic sixteen days, likely the best of our trip, but for now Europe was ready and waiting for us. We dug really deep into our bags to find socks, pants, and sweaters. It had been a while!

Venice was more beautiful than I expected for some reason. Sometimes you see so many photos ahead of time that when you actually get somewhere it's disappointing. But not Venice. We loved our day in Venice. The sun came out. We were free of plans and able to just wander and enjoy her lovely cobblestone alleyways and side streets, and gaze over bridges at passing gondolas on the busy waterways below. We skipped on taking a gondola ride as we have done with most major tourist attractions. 100 Euro wasn't in the budget for something we knew we wouldn't have felt we missed once we got home. No regrets there. What we could afford was carbonara. And gelato! That was a no-brainer and it was just as delicious as I had hoped. I chose coconut gelato and the boys, Nutella. Pizza, pasta, and gelato just taste different in Italy! There is no doubt about that.

Less than a day into our crazy train, bus, and automobile trip through Europe, we prepared to discover what backpacking was all about! Munich was up next, so after unpacking, doing laundry, and then repacking our backpacks, we loaded up and headed out. We arranged our drop off point as close as possible to the train station (a mere kilometre... ouch.) Since Australia, Rylan's backpack has been tossed into a cheap and gigantic rolling suitcase with a broken wheel that we've glued together three times. We acquired this along the way to pack all of our extra crap that doesn't have a home. He pulls that mammoth everywhere. Carson carries my beast and the rest of us are loaded to the hilt with our own backpacks and carry-on bags! It's quite the spectacle, but in true form, my family pulls it off like champs! We blew through that 1 km like nothing, made the train with plenty of time to spare, made friends with our overnight bunkmate (a lovely young guy from Texas en route to Berlin) and settled in for our uneventful overnight train trip.

CHAPTER 11

Italy

P acking up our rooms and preparing to say goodbye to our glorious cruise was much harder that we could have imagined. The boys had made great friends from all around the world. We had grown close to our special room steward and dining room servers from the Philippines, the leaders from the kids club, and our new Aussie friends for life Ty and Melissa. Sixteen days was the longest we'd been in one place (besides our in-laws home in Australia) and we had gotten quite settled. We paid another $30 CAD or so to have our huge bag of laundry washed. We packed our backpacks, said good-bye to Clint's large stash of ping pong medals, and met our friends for our final dinner and bon voyage visit.

We ported in Venice, Italy at 8:00 am Wednesday morning, April 20, 2017. Spring mornings in Italy can be cool or even cold. The days typically warm up under the Tuscan sun by the afternoon, which is how our day shaped up. We had spent the last six months predominantly in hot, humid, tropical climates and so the adjustment back to single-digit temperatures was jarring. I had booked our accommodation for our first three nights off the cruise at a caravan backpackers' collective called Camping Jolly. It was a short drive from the city and provided a free shuttle back and forth for shopping in the tourist hustle and bustle of Venice. The plan was to get settled and return later for just that! It had a restaurant and laundromat. The camping cabins were small and simple trailers that slept two people each and came with a bathroom. I had to book two but they were reasonably priced for Venice and beggars can't be choosers, especially beggars on a budget. We hailed an Uber minivan and made our way out of the city, excited for what the next few days would have in store. After our three nights in Venice, we had an overnight train booked to Munich, Germany for two nights, followed by an overnight budget-bus to Amsterdam. We would spend two nights there before moving our Amazing Race across the English Channel to the United Kingdom.

We arrived at Camping Jolly at around 9:00 am. As usual, it was too early to check in but they offered to store our bags and let us freshen up in the bathroom before we caught the shuttle to explore the lovely Italian marvel of Venice. We were dropped off about a block from the centre of Venice with instructions to meet our bus back there by 5:00 pm. Being Venice, it would have been romantic to stroll along the canals, enjoy a pasta dinner at sunset, followed by gelato or tiramisu for dessert, not to mention taking a gondola ride while being serenaded. But this was the real world and we weren't on vacation. The boys tired of walking almost instantly and the crowds were getting slightly overwhelming. The boys pestered me: *Where are we walking too? What's the destination? How much longer?* Finally we took a break and squished into a little canal cafe and splurged on fettuccine alfredo and pizza, of course! There were no washrooms available to the public so we wandered around aimlessly for what felt like hours until we found one that charged a few Euros per person and got in line. Welcome to Venice!

We moved on to the lineup at St. Mark's Basilica which was gorgeous, historic and completely worth the wait. I didn't know much about St. Mark's before our visit but a quick read up on it informed us that the building's structure dates back to the latter part of the 11th century. Much work has gone toward embellishing this, and the grand entrance has an ornamented roofline that is mostly Gothic. Gold mosaics cover most of the ground of the upper areas of the interior and took centuries to complete. The basic shape of the church has a mixture of Italian and Byzantine features, such as the marble floor, laid out in entirely geometric patterns and animal designs, installed in the 12th century. In the 13th century the external height of the domes was lifted by hollow drums raised on a wooden framework and covered with metal. The original ones are shallower, as we could see on the inside. The basilica really was a sight to behold and a photo could not do it justice, which didn't matter as we weren't allowed to take photos anyway.

It was getting time for gelato (in my opinion) so we made sure to indulge in one of my favourite treats before it was time to catch the shuttle back. Clint and the boys don't typically have sweet tooth's so they spend lots of time waiting outside of ice cream, gelato and custard places while I search for new and unique local flavours to write home about. We must have walked ten kilometres that day, so to say we were tired and had sore feet is an understatement. We made it back to our shuttle bus for the quick trip back to our cabin, enjoyed another pizza at the cafe, and went to bed.

The next day got off to a rough start when we woke to a very cold morning after none of us slept very well. The cabin walls were terribly thin, and the bathroom walls were adjacent to each other. Therefore, we had to listen to people coming and going to use the bathroom all night long. Because of the change in weather, it was clear Carson and Clint were going to need warmer clothes, mainly socks and hoodies. They Googled the closest mall, which ended up being a long walk, but walking was cheaper than Uber and a few hours later they returned and had found good deals on new hoodies and socks. I stayed back to do more laundry and the other two kicked a soccer ball around a little grass area outside, enjoying some quiet time to themselves. One of the coolest packing ideas I had come up with way back in Canada was to take the air out of Braden's favourite soccer ball and pack it with a small hand pump. Braden kept it with him the whole trip and pulled it out to play with many times!

When Clint and Carson returned, I decided to review our Germany plans. Originally I had booked an overnight train trip to Munich, thinking the experience would be fun without wasting a day travelling on the train. As it turned out, we pretty much got what we wanted from Venice the first day and didn't feel the need to head back into the city again. The boys were not interested in spending another day wandering, and Clint and I didn't want to waste the money. In hindsight, there was still a lot to still see and do in the area, but we didn't have a rental car and were still adjusting to the weather change. Probably, we were just missing the cruise life and not feeling up to it.

One problem was that the overnight train to Munich wouldn't leave until 9:00 pm, but the park had a strict noon check out. They offered for us to stay until 6:00 pm if we paid another night's stay for one unit. This was a huge pain now that we didn't feel like returning to Venice and my plan was starting to feel like a backfire. Clint was bored and questioning why I had booked a late-night train, disappointed that we would miss out on scenic Italian views by traveling at night. I rolled my eyes—I had confirmed that he was ok with this plan before I booked it. Unfortunately, in my attempt at efficient planning, I hadn't considered missing the scenery, which I too would have enjoyed. By this time I was starting to feel super frustrated. Not only were we spending more money to stay somewhere we were ready to leave, but we had to transfer all of our things from one unit into the other, which was barely big enough for three of us let alone five, for the rest of the day.

The weather was miserable, we were stuck inside, it was too late to change the train tickets, and the more I ruminated about missing the scenery while roughing it out all day in the tiny cabin with everyone underfoot, well, some might say I *lost it*. It was just one of those emotional days when we were all bickering and even after a few weeks I was *still* not feeling great health-wise. Clint took the boys out and left me alone to cry in frustration. On top of everything, I was starting to feel anxious about our arrival into Munich at 8:00 am since check in for that hotel wouldn't be until 3:00 pm. I started to worry about what we would do all day with our luggage and without a hotel room and a car. I had only booked one room with a maximum occupancy of four. It had looked like it could sleep five, but I knew Europe was strict about occupancy, and if we arrived early with all of our luggage there wouldn't really be a way to sneak anyone in. But three nights in Europe is a lot to have to spend on an extra room and I was, of course, trying to cut costs. The whole thing just felt *really* overwhelming all of a sudden. I took a nap, cleared my head, and decided to just make the best of it. What other option was there?

By 6:00 pm, we had repacked and loaded up in the shuttle to head back into Venice to catch the 9:00 pm train. Because we had a few hours to kill, we decided to eat dinner at the train station. It was about a kilometre walk from the shuttle to the train station, which I had already been worrying about, mostly for Carson who was still lugging around my gigantic fifty-pound top-heavy backpack. He insisted it was fine but I still worried he would meltdown. His moods were still mediocre at best and everyone's frustration levels were at an all-time high.

Before leaving Canada we had purchased expensive travel backpacks for everyone. Additionally, I had my purse and a carry-on, and the boys each had a large school binder with a carry handle. Originally, the plan was that I would carry all of the liquids and hygiene products and be the only one to pay for a checked bag. By Australia though, we realized that most long-haul flights didn't charge for checked bags, so I recruited a huge old throwaway suitcase from Jennine's cousin to throw all of the school binders in, the extra shoes that always seemed to be loose, and miscellaneous odds and ends. It was a good plan, only the suitcase was huge and old and had old wobbly wheels that I was certain would not last through a kilometre-long trek on the thousand-year-old cobblestone streets of Venice. But we ventured out anyway, hopeful and gaining excitement for Germany.

That was one *long* kilometre. I play the scene back in my head, wondering how chaotic and comical this Canadian family looked to the sophisticated and put-together Italians who witnessed us, loaded to the hilt with bags bigger than the boys themselves, traipsing awkwardly to the train station. The suitcase made it (thank goodness) but boy was it loud and goofy looking. And yes, Carson did have a mini-meltdown, which we expected, but not only did we reach the station, we made it early. First things first, we decided to find our train! We wandered billboard to billboard, trying to find the right platform for the 9:00 pm departure to Munich, without luck. We dropped our bags in a pile and left the boys to keep watch while Clint and I split up to scout them all out a second time. Still nothing. It was approaching 7:00 pm and we were starving, so against my better judgment, we held off on locating our train platform and split up to search for food. I continued wandering and even stopped by what looked like a ticket booth. I tried to ask the woman at the booth about our train, but she didn't know anything about departures or arrivals, and in broken English she told me to wait and the train would show up when it was supposed to. Or at least that's what I thought she said, I was kind of guessing.

By 8:00 pm a departure for Munechen appeared on the billboard. We hoped *Munechen* was Italian for Munich. Sure enough, right on time, our enormous overnight train to Munich, Germany, pulled in with fifteen minutes to spare. We loaded up yet again, located our train car, showed our tickets, and boarded our cubby hole for the night without a security search of any kind, or document verification, or luggage check. Nothing; just loaded straight onto the train. Shortly after, the stewardess did mention that the train would make a stop in the middle of the night as we crossed the German border so that the German police could check our passports, which indeed happened. I have no idea what time it was, but sometime after we drifted off to sleep, I was rudely awoken by a loud banging on our car door. I pulled it open and was blinded by a huge flashlight blaring into our cabin. I pulled out our passports that I had stashed under my pillow, handed them to the officer and reached my leg across to wake our cabin mate up. He had to show his as well. An officer rifled through them, said nothing, handed them back to the both of us, and away we went again!

Before sleep, we had spent the evening chatting away with our cabin mate, a young but fairly large down-home boy from Texas, USA. He had been backpacking through Europe and was on his way to meet up with his parents in Berlin. He was so thankful to have us for roommates and so were we; you never know who you could end up bunking with on these random excursions! We talked about the States, his school and family, our adventure, politics, and everything in between. Before long, as with all of our new friendships we had made along the way, we felt like we had made a friend for life. Unfortunately, in the shuffle to pack up in the morning we forgot to exchange contact information. He became, to us, "That guy from the States that we slept with on the train." Arrival into Munich was scheduled for 8:00 am, and as we watched green fields and German villages pass by, and eventually slowed to a crawl, it became evident that there was an icy blanket of frost on everything and we were about to face a significant adjustment in temperature yet again. We layered up with socks and hoodies, checked our phones to confirm that it was in fact -1 degree outside, and braced ourselves for chilly Munich, Germany.

Travel Tip - Don't be afraid to stay a little out of the city of Venice. There are many less expensive options and most offer free shuttle service in and back so it's a great way to save some money.

Blog Post: Early May

We arrived in Munich, Germany at 8:00 am and nearly died of what felt like freezing cold winter. It was only -1° but we'd been enjoying 30° weather for almost six months by this time. Two things were immediately clear: I needed at least a scarf, and my flip flops had to go! We quickly doubled up on sweaters and dug our socks and closed-toe shoes out of our packs. If there is anything we have been repeatedly grateful for on this trip, it is early hotel check ins, which haven't been a hassle at the fancy hotels we've been able to book with credit card points. I guess when you're Gold Elite, you get treated like gold!

We have found that when you take overnight trains and buses, not only do you need to arrange somewhere to spend the afternoon and early evening on the day of departure, but that arriving into cities at 6:00 or 8:00 am is not very practical either. So we found ourselves, yet again, showing up early and begging for a room. They accommodated us without hesitation! I'm still not sure exactly how we squeezed it all in, but for our first day in Munich we rented a car, drove out to Dachau Concentration Camp, toured the BMW Museum, and made it back to make it to Munich City Centre to stroll around Marienplatz Square before heading home to the hotel for bed. Not only that, but at some point, Clint and Braden raced over to watch a Bayern Munich soccer game! Sunday was another busy day, driving out into the picturesque Bavarian countryside; standing in a ridiculously long line in the cold and taking another long uphill hike to walk through a slightly disappointing Neuschwanstein Castle (aka Disney Castle from Sleeping Beauty), followed by a quick coffee and pastry stop in Fussen; and racing back to return the car and catch the overnight bus to Amsterdam. We received confusing and inaccurate instructions from two different people about where to catch the bus. That resulted in repeatedly racing back and forth through a very busy station, knocking over a bike and sending about ten more down in domino fashion, at which we stopped and stared in disbelief; what a farce! Barely going to make our bus, and now we have an entire row of bikes to stand up?

"Just go… just go," said a German lady who witnessed the whole thing. "This is Munich, just go. People ride bikes, they fall over! Just go, this is Munich!" she repeated.

Ok, thanks lady! Off we went with a laugh, a dozen bikes sprawled out on the ground in our wake, and found our station with moments to spare! Next stop Amsterdam… but not before ten hours on an overnight bus!

CHAPTER 12

Germany

It was so cold! We were shivering in our flip flops and lost yet again, trying to find transportation to our hotel. Finally, after several Ubers refused us because there were five of us, a desperate driver with a small van had mercy and let us pile in. It was a short and quiet ride to the Residence Inn Apartments located in East Munich. He dropped us off out front. To my dread, we arrived far too obviously and early to attempt a discreet shuffle in through a back entrance and the concierge wasted no time letting us know we could not sleep five people in one room. He did let us check in very early (credit card prestige to the rescue again!) and welcomed us to enjoy the breakfast that was still being served. He also informed me that they would be calling our room shortly to decide whether we would need an additional room or not. Shortly after we filed up to our apartment and unpacked, we received a call confirming that management decided we would need a second room. Drat! So King Carson packed his stuff up and was the lucky recipient of his own room for 3 nights. We had 2 queen beds and the other boys were used to being together and didn't want to split up, so they stayed. Carson was in heaven!

The free breakfast at The Residence Inn Munich East became known by me as the Best Hotel Breakfast of Our Whole Trip and My Entire Life. Previously, that title had been carried by the European breakfast included at Sparkling Hill Resort in Vernon, BC. If you've had that one, let me tell you: this was even better! It was a spread of a divine selection of german sausages, bratwurst and crispy bacon, gourmet pastries, several homemade preserves, a variety of cheeses, eggs, fruit, fresh pressed fruit juices, and self-serve lattes and cappuccinos. The all you can eat breakfast was the exact indulgence we all needed after a long night awake on the train and a busy day ahead in Germany. Unfortunately, it was also money mistake number three. What the concierge had failed to mention at check-in, and what we had failed to realize, was that free breakfast starts the morning *after* your first night, not the day you check in. That makes logical sense, because who checks into a hotel at 8:00 am anyway? Well, we were tired and starving and didn't think twice about it, so when he let us know we could help ourselves, we did just that. But when we were presented with the hefty bill of 25 Euro each, we just about died right there amidst our expensive, not-free pancakes. He had specified that the "hot" breakfast cost 25 Euro and the continental only cost 15; the difference between the two was basically meat. So of course we did what any cash-strapped parent on a strict budget does: a meat-eating inventory. *Did you eat bacon? Did you eat sausage?* and quietly, *Did he see you eat the hot stuff?* The scene unfolded so ridiculously, but with three of us eating at 25 Euro and two of us at 15 Euro, we spent a whopping 105 Euro. With tax, and a tip of course, we paid $160 CAD for free breakfast! Whoops! Welcome to Europe and welcome to travel!

I slept off our budget-breaking breakfast fiasco with a morning nap and Clint got to work trying to figure out what we were going to do in Munich, Germany for three days. We didn't have plans to rent a car but were aware of a Sixt location around the corner should we decide to. Braden had somehow got wind of a Bayern Munich futbol (soccer) game and begged Clint for tickets to go, which unfortunately had to be decided quickly as it was almost sold out. They were expensive and obviously not in the budget, but we had just blown $160 on breakfast so did a budget even exist anymore? Plus, it was unlikely they'd be back in Germany with an opportunity for this experience again. So, as a compromise, Clint decided that he and Braden would go to the game and the rest of us would do something else. Or nothing else, which was fine with me. My blog hadn't been updated for weeks and it would be nice to make some calls back home. So we mapped out all of our destinations for the weekend, bought futbol tickets, and Clint headed around the block to rent a BMW for us to explore Munich in. When in Germany, you drive what the Germans drive!

We zipped across the city to the BMW museum and spent the afternoon exploring a multi-level, ultra-modern walk through experience of the history of the BMW in Germany. The museum housed twenty-five exhibition areas including Future Forum, The Ultimate Sound Machine, Mini, and Rolls Royce exhibition areas, as well as simulated driving experiences and guided tours. For all my car-loving boys, it was exciting and extremely interesting. Everyone seemed to love it. The sun streamed in as the weather warmed, and admission was inexpensive which made it an enjoyable stop for all of us.

After that, we visited the Dachau Memorial Site. Dachau was established early as a concentration camp for political prisoners of The Third Reich. This camp served as the model for all later concentration camps and as a 'school of violence' for the SS men who controlled it. It existed for twelve years and over 200,000 men, women and children from all over Europe were imprisoned there and in its numerous sects. 41,500 people were murdered at Dachau and the day it was liberated by the US military on April 29th, 1945 over 30,000 completely enfeebled people were still imprisoned there, being held in squalor-like conditions, overtaken with hunger and disease. We learned that the murderous working conditions, the insufficient food rations, and the lack of hygiene facilities lead to a soaring death rate. It was initially planned to hold 6,000 people. In 1965, The Bavarian government established it as a memorial site called The Path of the Prisoners. We walked through the prisoner bath areas; the bunker which was one of the main areas for torture and extreme punishment; a former crematorium; the bunk houses where the prisoners slept; and many other memorials. We opted for a self-guided tour but Rylan insisted on a listening tour, so he went back for ear-buds and followed along on his own. It was a cool, overcast day which couldn't have reflected the somber mood any more appropriately. There was a lot of reading, typical of most museums, but the boys grew weary of it quickly so we took some photos and left after a few short hours. On the way out, I took a photo of the sign at the memorial's entrance and posted it to Facebook, finding it a fitting description of what we were reflecting on when we left the Dachau site.

May the example of those who were exterminated here between 1933 and 1945 because they resisted Nazism help to unite the living in the defence of peace and freedom and in respect for their fellow men.

Clint didn't waste one moment on that autobahn going any slower than he had to. Looking back, I don't even recall seeing a posted speed limit, but either way, he drove like the wind and loved every minute of it. We made it back to the hotel with lots of time to spare before Clint and Braden had to leave for the soccer game. I got to work updating my blog, and caught up on emails and planning next steps for the trip. The boys played games and rested to recover from our heavy afternoon. Later, Clint and Braden returned reeking of cigarette smoke and telling us hilarious stories of beer-filled futbol-loving German fans. All the crazy cheering and antics had left them in awe of how different a German soccer game is from a Canadian soccer game, definitely worth being there to witness in person! We wandered to a local grocery store before they closed for the evening and gathered enough ingredients to cook a simple dinner in our ramshackle kitchen as well as a supply of snacks for the next day. We were getting efficient at buying just what we needed to last us a day or two in even the most basic kitchen. Sometimes meals were elaborate, most of the time they were spaghetti and meatsauce, but they were always delicious.

The next morning we set out on a Bavarian road trip adventure to Neuschwanstein Castle, which famously had inspired Walt Disney's design of Sleeping Beauty's castle. It took us about two hours to drive there, through the rolling hills south of Munich and the picturesque countryside villages of the Bavaria Province of Germany. The weather was glorious for a road trip, warm with sunshine, and we were enamoured with everything we saw along the way. It was like driving through a scene from a childhood storybook. The only thing missing was Hansel and Gretel. We arrived at Neuschwanstein to cooler temperatures, patches of snow still on the ground, tour busses full of Asians, and admission lineups galore. Again, I unfortunately hadn't foreseen this. It wasn't even their busy season yet; *what did this place look like in the summer?* We regrouped, considered our options, and decided on joining the lineup as it seemed to be moving steadily. We bought our tickets for the walking tour and were kindly notified of a cute village nearby where we could kill some time before the tour would start a few hours later. We arrived at Fussen, Germany less than half an hour later, and decided to explore on foot. I was insistent on finding a German bakery for a coffee break, and it didn't take long as they were on every corner. What a perfect moment to cross 'Visit a German bakery in Germany' off of my bucket list!

It may seem like decisions are always seamless between Clint and I or that I come up with these great ideas on my own and he just comes along for the ride. But, no. That's not typically how it goes. We'd already tortured our children with our endless bickering and about what's important, what's valuable, and what's priceless. Everything, and I mean *everything*, is still, after twenty-some years together, a *discussion*. Sometimes we debate, sometimes we brawl, sometimes we just have a heated argument, but at a minimum, we always *discuss*. I love experiences. Clint loves some experiences, but he likes saving money more. In my mind, if we can't have experiences, then *why were we here?* Someone told us before we left that people travel the same way they live. Those who live extravagantly travel extravagantly; those who live frugally travel frugally. It was great advice to keep in mind while planning how much our year of adventure might cost. We lived fairly frugally and so I understood that's how we would travel too, but it became a negotiation to narrow down just how frugally. This day, I wanted treats at a German bakery, in a Bavarian village in the German countryside! So Clint obliged me and my bucket list whim, and we sat down to enjoy an indulgence. Coffee for us, hot chocolate for the boys, the most amazing cinnamon bun *für mich* (for me), and I got a perfectly posed photo to remember it all by.

We sauntered around Fussen, while the boys ran ahead, climbing railings, scaling old cobblestone ledges, and leaping around low-lying structures like they always do while exploring. We made it back without rushing for our afternoon tour, which included a fairly decent uphill winding walk to the castle. The boys ran ahead like usual, Clint took up the middle, and I lagged behind, slowing everyone down like usual. I had been feeling better but was still fighting a cough and some sinus congestion. The cool, crisp air and the hike made my lungs flare up leaving me winded. Clint's allergies had also suddenly appeared out of nowhere. In Canada, his allergies typically arrive around June and July, likely because of sage which grows all over Kamloops. But there was no sage to be seen in Germany and it was only late April, so whatever he was reacting to was unidentifiable, and his sniffling and sneezing was out of control and starting to wear him down.

While waiting among several large groups of people awaiting tours, our boys noticed how many people were smoking. This had become somewhat of a phenomenon to our Canadian-raised kids. They saw it in Fiji and Thailand where the culture was generally foreign anyway. Now, they were seeing it so prevalent in Europe too, strange against a more familiar cultural backdrop. We barely knew any smokers back home and rarely witnessed the ones we did know doing it since it was banned inside public places and even outside within six metres of doors and windows. So to see so many people puffing away with zero regard for the children in their midst was a surprise. The boys were very turned off by it.

Neuschwanstein Castle was a magnificent architectural feat, built by King Ludwig II of Bavaria in 1869, and was opened to the public shortly after his death in 1886. According to Wikipedia, 61 million people have visited the castle since, with up to 6,000 tourists visiting each day during the summer. Because of its secluded mountain top location, it survived destruction during both World Wars. For security reasons, unbeknownst to us until we arrived, the palace could only be visited on short guided tours, and there was no photography allowed at all. That was a huge disappointment, as was the massive size of our tour group, which made it near-impossible to see or hear anything unless you were in the first two rows. Overall, it was a unique and memorable experience and we were glad we made the effort to visit. However, we would hesitate to recommend going in a busier season, especially considering that it was expensive for what it was. We hit the autobahn for home. I knew Clint was speeding because he slowed to 100 km/hr and it felt like we were literally crawling. But I had no idea how fast we were actually going until I saw his Instagram later that night debuting the evidence with a cheeky smirk... 157 kms/hr—he's lucky it had been my afternoon nap time!

We still had time to squeeze in a quick jaunt over to Marienplatz Square when we returned to Munich. Marienplatz Square is a historic site built to celebrate the end of Swedish occupation. Today it is surrounded by both the old City Hall and the new City Hall, as well as numerous boutiques and restaurants. Marienplatz is famous for three weeks of Christkindlmarkt (Christmas market). People come from all around the world to experience German Christmas markets and I made a mental note to return one day to visit one. We left early as the pubs and restaurants were already booked for the evening, being that it was Saturday, and found a suitable non-smoking family friendly restaurant. It was a donair and fries place owned by a Lebanese couple who were overjoyed to seat and serve us. It wasn't traditional German food, which would have been a treat, but Germany had become multicultural just like Canada has, and it was reflective of the diverse restaurants available on any street corner in any major German city. We made a stop at an apothecary (pharmacy) for some allergy medicine for Clint, who was now under a full-fledged allergy attack. They didn't actually carry antihistamine medicine, which is typical for Europe, but sold us a homeopathic nose spray which helped immensely, and had him feeling better within a day. It was our final night in Munich, so we made use of the steam room and sauna at the hotel, packed up, and prepared for our journey to Amsterdam.

In the morning, we saved an expensive Uber ride by confirming with Sixt that we could return our BMW to a location closer to where our bus was departing. We loaded up the car, made it to the Sixt drop-off location easily enough, and got some simple directions for the walk to the bus station. However, life on the road has proven rarely easy, and of course we were given inaccurate directions to the Flex Bus station that we needed to reach within an hour. We wound up at a train station a few blocks over, and wandered around asking as many English-speaking Germans as we could find where the bus station might be. Nobody knew. Finally, Clint tracked someone down who sent us in a completely different direction, and with time ticking, we ran in that direction as fast as a family of five with three hundred pounds of luggage can run, but not without incident. As we ran past a long row of parked bicycles, Carson nudged one which sent them all crashing, like dominoes, to the ground. We all stopped dead in our tracks and gawked at the mess, dreading an attempt to start standing them back up and panicking about time. Out of nowhere a German angel-lady appeared.

"Just go, just go!! This is Munich, this is Munich! You just go!" She yelled at us, waving us off, guilt free.

"Thank you," I yelled back, and we continued on.

I guess in Germany, this happens regularly and apparently wasn't our fault, though it kind of felt like it was. Nonetheless, I was thankful to be let off the hook. Not a moment later, Flex Bus appeared out of nowhere inside a large, dusty, ramshackle warehouse. We had arrived on time and it had been cheap. That is all that mattered. We grabbed McDonalds from the food hall up the stairs, stowed our backpacks in the cargo stowage beneath the bus, and found our seats for our ten-hour overnight journey to Amsterdam. Munich was a success!

Travel Tip - Flex Bus is an inexpensive, safe and comfortable way to travel within Germany and between most European countries. Many come with WiFi, recliner seats, TVs and snack service. Just avoid overnight trips, sit back, relax, and enjoy the scenery!

Blog Post: April 2017

Amsterdam was on my list for Dutch history, the canals, croquettes, and of course tulips and windmills! What I may have overlooked was the red-light district and the cafes where pot-smoking is legal. Imagine my surprise during our very entertaining Sandeman's of Europe free walking tour when the guide 'educated' us on the 'illegal but tolerated' prostitution in Amsterdam. If only we had brought earplugs for the kids! I'm pretty sure Rylan missed the whole thing. Braden had a question or two. Carson though, understood it all! I can now confirm that yes, there are scantily-clad women standing in windows, literally displaying themselves for whomever is buying that day. Our instructions to the boys were clear: stare at the ground and don't look up until we tell you to! Thank God it was only a short, and early part of the tour. The rest was lovely, covering history, Anne Frank, canals, bridges, and architecture. It was a great tour and left us wanting more, but it ran late and duty to our schedule called. Clint took two boys to fetch our luggage from storage and locate the shuttle to our ferry while Braden and I crammed in a mediocre canal tour. We were sitting backwards, the windows were dirty, and the rush and money wasted on three unusable tickets left me stressed and frustrated with our planning. Also - we hadn't yet eaten that day! Braden and I ran from the tour to meet up with the others for the overnight ferry to England, tired, hungry, rushed, and stressed—oh, the travel life!

CHAPTER 13

Holland

By this time I'd come to understand why overnight trips are always cheaper. It's because they suck, and by this time I'd had my fill of them. At our age, Clint and I didn't feel a need to prove anything to anyone. Not that we'd ever had, but it seemed fun and whimsical at first to say we were taking the 'overnight train' or 'overnight bus' somewhere, but now the lustre had definitely been lost. We arrived like usual, dead-tired and feeling like trash with kinked-up backs and in desperate need of a toothbrush. We all chattered about our night and it turns out that I, shockingly, probably had slept the best. I had taken a melatonin and had ear plugs and an eye cover. Maybe I was just plain tired and in need of sleep, who knows? Carson and Clint hadn't slept at all. It was dreadful to hear our bus driver on his PA system grunting out instructions, smacking his lips into the microphone, and droning on with a thick German accent. Not only did I underestimate how many times we would stop and start on this brutal journey, but I also hadn't considered that we'd be listening to the driver grunting out SO LOUDLY at every single stop made throughout the night. It was awful.

I woke with a start around 3:00 am, wondering how we could know that no one was stealing our luggage. We were one of the last ones on, meaning our luggage was front and centre, meaning also that each person disembarking in the night potentially had the opportunity to take ours. I was so rattled about it but realized there wasn't anything I could do, so I put it out of my mind and tried to fall back to sleep. Sometimes life just has to run on the honour system.

We arrived in Amsterdam, Holland at 8:00 am, hoping for a nearby Uber and praying that we could check in to our hotel early again. We tracked down a ride, settled on the cost, and off we went. Amsterdam was just waking up for the day; a much different sight than any other city we had experienced in the morning. It was, by all appearances, a modern and very green city with loads of lush landscaping as far as the eye could see, and bicycles everywhere. Munich had been a bicycle city, but this was a bicycle heaven. The Aloft Amsterdam allowed us to check in early thanks to our points prestige. We were also offered room upgrades and gladly accepted two rooms with partial kitchens and beds that felt like clouds.

It looked like it was going to be another cold day in Europe and Rylan was feeling down. He had bounced back for a couple weeks but the overnight trips were wearing on all of us and I assumed he just badly needed some sleep. So, sadly, we passed on venturing out that day. It kind of felt like a wasted day but I knew if we didn't prioritize rest, all the missing sleep might bite us in the butt later. I was overjoyed to see that our hotel was adjacent to a yummy-looking Dutch restaurant as well as a mall and grocery store, so we didn't really need to go out anyway. After popping over to the adjacent restaurant for Dutch croquettes and a burger, we returned to sleep the morning away. I woke up first, deciding to head out for some groceries. We only planned to stay two nights, but we had a sufficient kitchen between our two rooms and I knew we would be able to find something appropriate to cook. If nothing else, we could always rely on spaghetti and meat sauce.

During the beginning of our trip, I loved the grocery stores. I loved the variety of new and interesting foods, I loved the cheaper-than-Canadian prices, and I loved the challenge of deciphering a new language and identifying new ingredients. I still enjoyed it but by now could feel the love waning. Europe was expensive on the whole because of our terrible exchange rate. Even though groceries were reasonable, costs always added up. I was thankful to be at the grocery store alone and able to price check and put some thought into what we could cook in a limited kitchen. Surprise, surprise, we did end up with the usual spaghetti and meat sauce. It's the easiest and cheapest meal to cook on the road. I threw in a garlic loaf and a bagged salad, and managed to find strawberries, bananas and chocolate to treat us to a fondue dessert. That's how you feed a family of five in Europe for 35 Euro! I even stopped by the candy store on my way back for some famous Dutch candy. We devoured dinner and then spent a few hours trying to figure out how we were going to cram our Amsterdam activity wish-list into one measly half day. Sadly, we weren't able to. Our ferry to Newcastle was scheduled to board the next day at 4:00 pm and we still needed a half hour or so to get to the port. So I did what I always did, starting with scouring Groupon for deals and checking Sandman's online to see if they had any available free walking tours. I was excited to find one opening remained for 11:00 am for a ninety minute tour. That would leave us enough time to burn over for an hour-long canal tour of Amsterdam at 1:00 pm, and then grab our stowed luggage in time to catch the bus. It was an optimistic plan, but we were all on board with it. I had to figure out what to do with all our luggage for the day. Turns out, luggage storage is an actual thing in Amsterdam. We clearly weren't the first people to need it nor would we be the last. I used Google maps to locate one closest to our walking tour that was also near the end-point of our canal tour. I cringed to see that it was going to cost about 50 Euro but we didn't have a choice if we wanted to see Amsterdam, and such is life so I booked it. I bought tickets from Groupon for a canal tour for our family of five, I booked the free walking tour, I booked the bus to the port, and we were all set for our fun day in Amsterdam! That was Plan A. You can never count on Plan A.

The next morning found us behind schedule from the start after our Uber mysteriously pulled up, and then took off again before Clint could confirm it was our ride. We were left scrambling on the sidewalk in the rain with all of our things. We found another ride but it put us way behind, and of course I was annoyed that Clint hadn't made more of an effort to let the driver know who we were. We arrived in central Amsterdam and had a very difficult time finding the luggage storage place, causing further delays. We were about to be very late for our walking tour, if it hadn't already left without us, and I had to use the bathroom. I knew I might not get another chance with the rest of the day being on a tight schedule. I ran into the closest McDonald's for the restroom while Clint ran ahead trying to hold the tour. I made it without a moment to spare, or to collect my thoughts, or even a real chance to take in the majesty of central Amsterdam. What

I do remember is a lot of people, pigeons, and rain. Someone in the group pointed out that Justin Bieber owned the $27 million penthouse flat of one of the buildings overlooking the Dam Square neighbourhood where we were gathered. All we could see from the ground was floor to ceiling windows and it looked like it was under some kind of construction. Of course it was—$27 million and it needs a reno! *Brat,* I thought and got back to focusing on what our tour guide was educating us on.

The tour started with a headcount in the pouring rain. We were ill-equipped for the cold and wet without even an umbrella since we'd had no time to think ahead. It never ceases to amaze me that we remembered to pack for specific situations, but *never* remember to take those things with us *in* those situations. Things such as umbrellas in the rain, water shoes for the rocks, wind coats when it's cold, kleenex when we have sniffles or allergies etc. Just another annoyance that I had to try to avoid dwelling on after it occurred to me.

Our amazing tour guide was well-educated, and clearly excited to be there, cheery under the cover of his umbrella, schooling us on Amsterdam culture and history. We strolled the Red Light District where the boys were instructed to keep their eyes on the ground. We learned about how the Dutch take such pride in being diverse and acceptable of all things in a 'don't ask, don't tell' kind of way. We learned that coffee shops are actually pot shops as we strolled and admired the gorgeous architecture of buildings, canals, and dykes. We sauntered past cheese shops, bakeries, and pubs galore. It was entertaining and informational and I wish we could have enjoyed it with less rush. We sauntered past the Anne Frank house and heard about how the line to get in was over 1 km long most days in the summer. I wished we had been able to see it. Someone else mentioned the tulip fields just outside of Amsterdam and how gorgeous they were to see in the spring. It felt like we barely scratched the surface of what could be seen and done in Holland, and Amsterdam in particular. Once we had booked our condo in Cancun, Mexico, everything else leading up to that had to fit in the timeline so we really only had the time that we had. I was feeling frustrated by that too. Watching the time now, I mentioned to Clint repeatedly that we needed to leave early to get to the boat. We had no idea how long the walk was going to be and hadn't eaten anything in several hours. Time was ticking. Clint was loving the tour and not feeling the pinch in the same way that I was. I tried waiting it out but was feeling desperate about possibly missing the boat. At 12:30 pm I put my foot down and demanded that we get going. We left a donation with the tour guide and began our amazing race through central Amsterdam to the canal tour.

By the time we arrived the lineup was a mile long, just as I had predicted it would be. We had purchased tickets but they were first-come first-served and we both knew we weren't going to make it onto the 1:00 tour. We discussed under duress and frustration and made the decision that Braden and I would take the next tour while Clint took the other two boys to retrieve all of our luggage on their own and figure out where we were supposed to meet the bus for the ferry to NewCastle. It meant three wasted canal tickets that had been expensive, and left me crying and stressed about making it back in time for the bus ourselves. We were the last ones loaded onto the boat tour. The windows were filthy and somehow we were seated backwards making it very difficult to see anything. We tried to be positive and not focus on the time. I was frazzled and annoyed at how badly the day had gone. It was all I could do not to focus on how much better it would be if only we had left when I wanted to. We arrived back with ten minutes to find the rest of our gang and load our things on the bus. On the way out of the city I remembered we'd forgotten to buy our souvenir magnet, and by then it was too late; another Amsterdam disappointment. But, my swift-thinking hubby redeemed himself when he pulled a small paper bag out of his pocket. To my surprise he had remembered! The day was a giant stressful blur and we were all starving, but we made the bus on time and we had our token magnet! The ferry to The United Kingdom was calling our name!

Travel Tip - Aloft from Marriott Hotels has the BEST beds! And go to Holland! It is magical and highly underrated.

Blog Post: Early May 2017

Venice, Munich, and Amsterdam are checked off the bucket list! Really though, we feel we would need a return trip to each city to really experience them. These European destinations had to be squeezed into a predetermined window of our itinerary, set between the date the cruise ended and our deadline to arrive in Mexico. We loved Europe and left with a desperate feeling that we had missed so much, but also feeling forever grateful for what we had been able to see. The overnight ferry from Amsterdam connected us to Newcastle, England via the English Channel. The water was wavy, making for a bumpy night. Thank God for a medicated sleep through the worst of it! It was an expensive night too, as it cost $20 CAD just for a burger. We were quite glad to reach land.

Newcastle is old, beautiful, and welcomed us with cold rain and our first English breakfast though we skipped the black pudding. Yet again we received terrible directions to our car rental lot. So off we trudged, tired and lost in the rain, and still feeling a little disjointed from our rough night. After me stressing to bits, which sadly seems to be my regular response to situations like this, the boys dropped our bags and went in opposite directions, each annoyed and determined to find this silly place! Clint was the lucky one, having finally reached the agent by telephone. We loaded up again in the rain and trooped off like pack rats! Hours later we were fed and watered, had new currency, and a new car with GPS. Finally, we drove off into the most enchanting English countryside along the coast. We made our way through the hills, past lake cottages and majestic castles to Scotland! Sometimes it seems as though nothing comes easy with travel, but it is always rewarding if you can just hang on!

Our apartment for two nights in Edinburgh was perfect and had everything we needed including a lovely view. It was close to Walmart for groceries and a local mall where we got a phone plan and enjoyed a fun stop at Pound Mart, like Canada's The Dollar Store, only this Pound Mart is true-to-name with everything priced at a pound or less. We got shampoo, razors, bandaids and other random junk that we thought would come in handy. We walked away with two bags and it cost 12 pounds (around $18 CAD). We settled in easy and Scotland was off to a great start!

We spent the next two days exploring castles, studying history, and driving the Scottish countryside. Clint checked an item off his bucket list when we ventured out to St. Andrews, where golf originated. He was like a kid in a candy store! After touring Edinburgh Castle we walked a portion of the Royal Mile, which is the main thoroughfare of Edinburgh, and then hit the road again, heading to Liverpool, England. We planned an overnight stop in Liverpool as it was our halfway point to Wales, where we planned to see old friends. We arrived late, crammed in dinner at the mall, and crashed early. Our European amazing race was starting to take its toll, on me in particular. All of us still had coughs, clearly fighting whatever bug we had caught on the cruise, and the cold windy air wasn't helping us get better. Exhausted, I didn't have enough energy to do anything in Liverpool. Clint squeezed in a quick visit to The Beatles Cafe in the morning and brought me a delicious pumpkin spice latte in a fun Beatles cup so I could take a token Liverpool photo.

CHAPTER 14

Scotland

Boarding the ferry was similar to embarking on a cruise: waiting in long line ups; repeatedly having to show our IDs; packing into overfull elevators; and fumbling around long narrow corridors to find our room. I had booked a family room that came with five pull-down twin beds, a basic cubby bathroom and a small window. The ferry would sail the English Channel overnight. We would arrive in Newcastle, England at 8:00 am from there we would shuttle into the town centre, find our rental car and then make our way to Scotland. I was well aware by this point that plans change, but that was the plan. Alas, I never managed to get into a Plan B mindset and too often let my frustration get the best of me. I wish I could adjust more quickly and easily whenever plans do not go my way.

In preparation for what we might encounter in 'a la ferry' life, I had Googled restaurants and meal plan options ahead of time. Meal plans were outrageously, and unnecessarily, expensive or so I thought at the time. I had also planned on getting an early dinner in Amsterdam before we boarded hoping both to enjoy some local Dutch delicacy and to avoid having to buy food on the ship, but we'd been too hurried and unable to find a moment to eat. So, after we settled into our cabin, we went in search of food and to figure out how to spend the evening on this baby beast of a ship. The formal restaurant was obviously out because of price, so we opted for burgers and fries at the casual bistro. As it turned out, a meal of burger and fries with a drink rang in at a crippling 25 pounds, about $43.00 CAD. Each! We sighed and ordered what we needed and not a morsel more, wishing we were American or Omani or from anywhere else really, other than Canada. The Canadian dollar sucked everywhere and the exchange felt constantly defeating. The kids found a theatre playing a current movie, and it cost a fortune like everything else on the cash-sucking ship. Clint and I were feeling frustrated and tired of saying no, so we sent the boys to the movie with popcorn money too, and were just glad for a couple hours of peace and quiet. I wandered into a gift shop out of sheer boredom and found a lovely scarf that somehow was a decent price and bought it for myself. We still hadn't adjusted to the cooler climate. I was always cold and hadn't brought enough warm enough clothes for outdoor activities unless the UK magically warmed up while we were there. I was so glad for my beautiful little find and addition to my weary wardrobe.

Just before bed the captain announced over the loudspeaker that it would be clear sailing across the passageway and we should arrive right on time the next morning. It took me a while to fall asleep as the waves had us seriously rocking long before I could even attempt to doze off. Thank God I don't get seasick, and thank God that Clint had already fallen asleep because he does! Even so, it was awful. Just when I thought the rolling around in my bunk couldn't get worse, it would. At one point I sat right up and looked around to see if the movement was as extreme as it felt. The boys on top bunks were an inch away from being thrown right off every time the room tipped back towards me. I couldn't believe my family were all sleeping soundly through the mayhem. I finally managed to be swayed to sleep sometime in the middle of a long night and woke to clear skies and calm waters. We repacked and spent *two hours* in the check out line, only to be told we had been waiting in the wrong line. As international travellers, we could have just walked off ahead of the line of Brits! That would have been nice to know ahead of time. The bus was already waiting outside to take us to Newcastle. We were excited to have our feet on land and definitely felt ready for breakfast.

During the bus ride into town we tried to locate the car rental place on Google maps so we could determine how far we would have to carry our things, but couldn't manage to find it. We even asked the bus driver if he knew where Enterprise car rental was. He seemed to think it was across and down the street from our drop-off, but was unsure and more or less brushed us off. We headed across the street from the Newcastle central train station and hoped for the best. We wandered back and forth looking for signs in confusion about how best to proceed. *Should we eat in this tourist trap now and worry about renting a vehicle after? Should we keep looking and then drive for breakfast later? Should we walk in the general direction we've been given and hope something appears?* The boys were hungry and I was annoyed that all of this was feeling so difficult. How hard could it be? We tried calling several times but there was no answer.

Eventually, a passerby had mercy on us, indicating that we only had one block further to go, but that we'd have to keep our eyes peeled because Enterprise would be around a corner. We crossed through into an industrial area and it became obvious that we were on the wrong track again. The wind and the rain started on cue, we had no shelter, and I just wanted to cry. Clint and the boys dumped all the luggage at my feet and divided up to search, determined to find this place come hell or high water. An agent finally answered the phone and confirmed we were in the right area, but that we'd have to double-back to where we started, then walk another block in the opposite direction. We finally landed at the office of Enterprise Car Rental, more than ready to get our car and bolt! Except... surprise! Our car wasn't ready yet! The agent sent us back to the train station for breakfast, saying she hoped to get us on the road within a couple of hours. So we trekked back, ate an expensive English breakfast of beans and toast and even tried a bite of black pudding. It was the first time, and the last time, that we did. So gross! We received notice that our car was ready around 11:00 am, raced back for the keys, loaded up and hit the motorway to Scotland! Though not before Clint stalled several times trying to get us out of downtown Newcastle at lunch hour on a Monday. It was mildly terrifying but we laughed hysterically every time it happened and I just prayed he didn't get us killed. He was driving a standard on the wrong side of the road, on the wrong side of the car, with a left-hand shifter. I have no idea how he pulled it off but he did. Clint was an awesome British driver... once we got out of town.

The drive between Newcastle, England and Edinburgh, Scotland was a breathtaking array of seaside cliffs; rustic, narrow, windy country roads; beaches under a hazy skyline with roaring thunderous waves; ancient majestic castles; and quaint English villages with cobblestone streets and red phone booths. I was finally breathing fresh air and able to take it in again. We drove through scenes we'd only experienced in the movies. It was absolutely glorious and it took everything in us not to stop every five minutes for photos and views, each better than the last. We stopped to check out an ancient, abandoned castle, wandering the perimeter while the boys ran to explore inside the broken rock walls. They waved down at us from the top while we stood in awe of the grandeur of its construction. We took in as many sights as we could while keeping an eye on the clock. It was difficult to keep moving, but we needed to make it to Edinburgh within three hours so we could check in to our condo before the main office closed. Clint loves castles and history and these stops increased his excitement to see what experiences Edinburgh had to offer. We arrived and checked in for a weekend stay in a cute two-bedroom seaside apartment. It was too late for groceries so we found a family restaurant close to where we were staying and had dinner before stopping at the nearby Asda (UK Walmart) to stock up for a few days' worth of food.

The next morning it was Clint's turn to check an item off his bucket list; his dream of stepping foot on to St. Andrews golf club and course. We drove two hours into the Scottish countryside through roadside villages and wide expanses of farmers' fields scattered with sheep. We passed castles and ruins, lakes and ponds. The sun was shining and it couldn't have been a more beautiful day for a drive.

Clint started golfing early in our marriage and it soon became a deep-seated passion that he pursued relentlessly. His clubs came with us on just about every trip we've ever done, and we started referring to them as 'the girlfriend.' He had brought them with us to use in Fiji and Australia, but sold them before leaving Australia—as was his plan—because they were an older set. So, although he didn't have plans to golf, he and golfers worldwide agree: you don't come to Scotland and not go to St. Andrews. St. Andrews has a history over six hundred years old, and is known worldwide as the home of golf. It has six amazing courses in total but the so-called *Old Course* is so famous that it costs hundreds of dollars to play, and tee times often need to be booked months ahead. It's set at the outskirts of St. Andrews village which is a small town and includes an ancient cathedral which was once the largest church in Scotland, and a prestigious, world-renowned University and St. Andrews Castle which is an attraction in and of itself. Along the streets boutiques, pubs, and cafes overlook the Atlantic Ocean. It was absolutely gorgeous and a photo could never do it justice, but we sure tried.

We only had two days in Scotland but the admission prices to castles that were managed by the government, or that had been privately restored, were quite expensive. We found a deal on a pass that the cashier at St. Andrews Castle sold us. The Scotland Heritage Pass gave us unlimited admission to most of the well-known castles and other tourist stops. We hadn't really planned the rest of our day or the following day so it was nice to have the option of seeing most of them for free. Clint headed into the golf museum while the rest of us ate lunch and wandered. He wanted to buy a souvenir for his golf bestie, who also happened to be managing our accounting and mail for us while we were away, so we found the golf gift shop and bought a few signature St. Andrews treasures to surprise him with. We spent the rest of the afternoon exploring the castle and cathedral and just wandering the village, with no particular rush to be anywhere else in the world.

After checking to see what other interesting places we might want to take in using our Heritage Pass, we decided on Loch Leven Island which happened to be just a small detour on our route home. After paying for our tickets in a cute lakeside ticket booth, we got to ride in a small motor boat across the lake to the island where we were dropped off. We had the place all to ourselves to explore! Loch Leven was the castle where Mary Queen of Scots was held captive for a month in 1567 before escaping with help from the castle-owner's brother. The story is an intriguing one, and the boys enjoyed scaling the castle ruins.

We climbed the stairs to call out to each other across the meadows between old walls. The boys ran around in the grass. I took one of my favourite photos of the entire trip at Loch Leven. The boys climbed as high as they could from the inside and each perched themselves facing out an old window-opening. I took the photo from below. Looking back, it was very high and not even remotely secure, leaving very little room for error. But, we were having such a great time that I think we all got a little lost in the moment. Before long, the boat arrived back to return us to land.

We were tired from the day, certainly too tired to cook, so we stopped on the way home for Scottish Chinese food take-out which was different, but not in a way we could pinpoint, from Canadian Chinese food. It was just as delicious though. In fact, we agreed it might even be *better* than the Canadian version. It was time, yet again, to do the laundry and I was thankful our apartment came equipped with a washer and dryer. We rounded everything up and spent the evening reorganizing, washing, and trying to dry our clothes in time to head out in the morning. I kept putting the loads back in the dryer, but even after everyone else went to bed, I still couldn't get anything to dry properly. We couldn't pack up damp clothes in the morning, so I found a space heater in the closet, laid all the clothes out throughout the hallway and living room and left them to dry, feeling extremely frustrated and just hoping they would be dry enough to pack by the morning.

The next day the laundry was wrinkly but at least dry, so we shook everything out, folded it up as best we could, and packed. The plan was to stop in Edinburgh to walk the Royal Mile, continue on as far as Liverpool where we had booked another apartment for the night, and then carry on to Wales for three nights staying with friends, before finally heading to London. We found the cheapest and closest place to park and made the uphill journey to explore the main attraction of Scotland: Edinburgh Castle and the Royal Mile.

Edinburgh Castle stands over four hundred feet above sea level on a volcanic crag called Castle Rock, overlooking the city of Edinburgh. A quick search on Wikipedia informed us that Castle Rock has been the site of human activity for at least three thousand years, was twice captured by English invaders, and twice retaken by the Scots. The last monarch to stay overnight in Edinburgh Castle was Charles 1, in 1963. Today it is one of Scotland's most popular tourist attractions, and historical markers and signage throughout the castle informed us that it also houses the oldest crown jewels in the UK; the Stone of Destiny, which is an ancient symbol of the Scottish Monarchy; and the National War Museum of Scotland. We walked through St. Margaret's Chapel from the 12th century, as well as many restored living quarters, the Great Hall, the Half Moon Battery, underground bunkers, and a prison. The castle was an architectural marvel. We finished the morning cruising the Royal Mile which is the mile that runs between the main castle and the palace, made up of streets like Castlehill, the Lawnmarket, the High Street and Abbey Strand. It is the busiest street in the Old Town and is an eclectic mix of shops, restaurants, pubs and visitor attractions. It was both mesmerizing and exhilarating.

Unfortunately, our next destination was a half-day's drive away and we knew if we didn't hit the road soon, we'd be sorry later. We stopped for lunch a short distance into our trip. We discovered that the roadside stops were really amazing in the UK. They pop up every hour or so and include clean public washrooms, gas, snack stores, gift shops, and a full food court offering a variety of culinary options plus outside eating areas. They were a lovely and welcome relief after a few hours on the road. We found our apartment in Liverpool (the home of the Beatles) by about 5:00 pm. I had just enough energy left to grab dinner at the adjacent mall and was asleep by 8:00 pm, exhausted by the last few continuously busy days and late nights. My sinuses were still bugging me and I was still not feeling 100% better. Clint got up bright and early, eager to check out the Beatles cafe. I slept in while he grabbed me a pumpkin spice latte in a signature Beatles cup for my token Liverpool photo! I texted our friends in Wales to let them know we were on our way and we hit the highway again. We couldn't have been more excited to see our people.

> **Travel Tip - Buy the Scotland Heritage Pass if you're interested in Castles and have a few days. They were available at any major attraction and a great way to see a lot on a budget.**

CHAPTER 15

Wales

I will always remember the day back home that our neighbour Dianna texted to let me know we had new neighbours moving in, coming all the way from Wales. It was the summer of 2014 and she had invited them over for afternoon tea; they had a son around the same age as Braden and Rylan who hadn't met any kids in the neighbourhood yet. So we all ended up in her backyard that day, meeting our new neighbours who would go on to become dear friends. The boys and Joseph became inseparable. Whenever he wasn't sleeping at our house, they were sure to be at his. The only time he went home was to eat, so maybe he wasn't fussy for my Canadian cooking. They lived on our street, Nechako Drive, for a year and then moved a couple of blocks away because of landlord issues, but the boys continued to spend every waking moment together.

One of our saddest days as a family was when we had to say goodbye to our dear friends. Unfortunately, Canada had been tough on them. Aldo's job hadn't panned out, and after Maria had spent too many weeks home alone with the kids they made the very difficult decision to move back to Wales. At the sombre goodbye party, I gifted them a bronze maple leaf car hanger decoration as a Canadian memento. We presented Joseph with a copy of our house key and reminded him that he was always welcome; our home would always be his home too. At the time, we had been keeping our business deal and travel plans on the down low, but Aldo and Maria were in on it as they had become close to us. When they left, I promised them that if and when we made our trip happen, we would make sure to visit them in Wales. I'm a woman of my word, so as soon as we knew our travel dates from London to Mexico I worked the plan backward to figure out the approximate dates that we could be in their area. They had been so excited when I texted them, and exclaimed that they couldn't wait to see us. Those dates happened to be a long weekend for them, so the timing couldn't have been more perfect.

We found their house easily, arriving around 3:00 pm. Joseph had grown a foot taller and his voice had deepened, but nothing much else had changed. For the most part they had just picked up where they left off when they returned to Wales, and had recently moved into a lovely new home in a brand new neighbourhood in Swansea. The sadness of having to leave Canada was still with them, for Aldo especially. The move had been a lifelong dream of his, and for it to have fallen apart was grievously frustrating for him. As soon as we arrived, the boys grabbed a soccer ball and were gone in an instant. They had still been gaming together and FaceTiming, so being together felt just like old times. We hugged our friends and settled into their home. They insisted we stay in their master bedroom, which we argued about, but to no avail. They ordered an Indian feast for dinner our first night, which was absolutely delicious. It was just so nice to be with them and to catch up. We're all such easy company together that it was as if no time had passed at all. Maria's sister Helen stopped by later in the evening as she had somewhat of an itinerary planned for the weekend but wanted to know what kinds of things we liked doing. We had met her a couple of times on her visits to Canada and being the traveler that she is known to be, was nominated most qualified to show us around. We looked over all of her suggestions and decided on visiting castles, the beach and an underground mine that was one of the most popular tourist attractions in the area. And, admission was free, which of course was a bonus.

The next morning we headed out for our first big day exploring Wales. It was a cold and rainy day so gearing up with safety equipment and a headlamp to descend hundreds of feet into Big Pit Mine was probably the best thing we could have done; at least it was dry. It was cold and dark in the pit and I may have been scared once or twice, but the history was super interesting and it was especially fun to experience with friends. Big

Pit is Wales' oldest working mine. Aldo was worried that it wasn't a very 'Wales' thing to do, but we loved it, just happy to be there and to be with friends. Joseph had a favourite trampoline park that he wanted to take the boys too, so we dropped them off and walked next door to Costa, a popular coffee chain, to wait for them while enjoying an afternoon coffee and tea. We couldn't be in Wales without having fish and chips so we stopped at Rossi's for dinner and afterwards tried a Wales original, Joe's Ice Cream Parlour for the "World's Best Ice Cream" with their signature wafer. Our first Wales outing did not disappoint.

Helen returned our second morning and had planned out a lovely day for all of us. Carson wasn't feeling great again and, I assumed, was getting tired and needed some alone time. He was still cranky most days and even though he loved being with our friends, he was missing home. Frankly, I was tired of him frowning in every family photo and things could be quite a bit lighter when he wasn't around, so we decided it was fine for him to stay home alone for the day.

Our first stop was Caerphilly Castle, the largest castle in Wales. It was built by an invading Norman lord in 1268 and then destroyed by a Welsh prince two years later. The following year, 1271, it was rebuilt bigger and stronger but by the 17th century one of its famous towers began to lean. Coal millionaires spent years in the 19th and 20th centuries restoring it to the tourist attraction that it is today. Besides Edinburgh Castle, Caerphilly was the largest and most intact castle we had visited yet. We climbed a million stairs and walked from tower to tower while the boys ran around. It was such a fun and laid back way to spend the morning and this unique experience was not lost on me.

No experience had been, yet. I tried to stay in the moment as much as I possibly could, taking in every sight, smell, sound, texture and taste of the lands we visited, searing them into my memory and quietly thanking God for the opportunity to be on a journey that I had begged him for. Even on our most difficult or frustrating days, and no matter how many times my meticulous plans went up in smoke, I still never wished we'd stayed home or be back home. Never once. Travel was feeding a hunger in my soul, nourishing my heart and bringing my dreams to fruition. I loved the adventure and promise of something new and different always around the next corner. I savoured the moments, knowing they would soon be memories. Life on the road never got monotonous, seldom stayed comfortable, and challenged me every day, in multiple ways. That was the joy of it. God met me wherever I was in the world and I never lacked. I tried not to think of when or how it would end, and avoided the 'what will we do when we get home' conversation like the plague. It was a question that pursued us relentlessly; we couldn't blame people who were just curious. But, the truth was that *we didn't care* what would happen after the trip. The trip was all there was. We'd shrug off questions and redirect conversation back to the present locale. The present was all that ever mattered, and that's how both Clint and I wanted it.

Leaving the castle, we detoured to Swansea by the sea for lunch on the pier. We took fun photos of the boys down by the water, running beachside and climbing rock faces back up to meet us. We made it home for dinner and Aldo cooked us an Italian feast (his heritage) of spaghetti carbonara and garlic bread. Our time together was coming to another sad end. We stayed up late drinking warm Ovaltine and watching TV while the three boys all piled into Joseph's king bed upstairs and played video games until the wee hours. We finished up our laundry, packed, and loaded up our car for our final journey in the UK. Aldo had to leave late that night in order to return to his worksite by the next morning, so we said our goodbyes before the rest of us headed to bed. We felt so thankful that we made this part of the trip happen and couldn't have appreciated the Welsh hospitality more. We left Wales blessed beyond measure.

Travel Tip - Find a Joe's Ice Cream, it really is The World's Best!

Blog Post: Late May 2017

London was the least memorable of our European stops. Our afternoon spent in Bath, England, before our arrival in London was, however, the most memorable part of our final journey through the UK. There, we toured the old Roman baths, and enjoyed lunch and a divine walk around a gorgeous village. We arrived in London late, cold, tired, and with only one day to cram in whatever we could. It was a ridiculously painful two-hour drive into City Centre (though only 28 miles.) We arrived very late for our walking tour and departed early, disappointed in the content. Lunch was expensive. The entire day had a soundtrack of police sirens and overhead helicopter patrols, even drowning out our tour guide at times. We took some token photos in front of Buckingham Palace and wandered back to our car with a blasé, been-there-done-that kind of feeling. This was an average day in London our guide said... sheesh! I know we somehow missed out but, we were there and got some good photos. We were more than ready to get back to the hotel. A great new friend we had made in Fiji but who lived in London met us at our hotel for a good visit. It was a fun reunion and nice to share stories about how our respective journeys had gone. Another wonderful reward of travel has been to gain new friends everywhere!

Our flight to Mexico left early the next day and was as enjoyable as an eleven-hour flight could be! I was still coughing, unfortunately, and we were all exhausted from late nights, long drives, early mornings, and lack of routine. We were definitely ready to relax in Mexico. The hot beach was calling our names!

CHAPTER 16

England

London was difficult and not our favourite stop by any stretch of the imagination. The drive from Wales to London took three hours and there were many places along the way that we would have loved to tour, had we the time. We chose Bath, England, the main reason being that it came highly recommended. Driving into Bath was breathtaking and I knew immediately we had made an amazing choice. Bath is the largest city in the county of Somerset, and is known for its Roman-built baths.

The area was given the Latin name Aquae Sulis (the waters of Sul) in 60 AD when the Romans built a grand bathing and socializing complex, although hot springs (healing waters) were known even before then. Because of its cultural and historical significance, the city became a World Heritage Unesco site in 1987 which also granted it legal protection. In 2012, a hoard of 30,000 silver Roman coins (believed to date from the 3rd century) were found about 450 feet from the Roman baths. The brochures at the entrance to this ancient site and spa described it well: "Built for pleasure and relaxation, beautiful Bath has been a wellbeing destination since Roman times. The healing waters are still a big draw, both at the ancient Roman Baths and the thoroughly modern Thermae Bath Spa, which houses the only natural thermal hot springs in Britain that you can bathe in. It's honey-coloured Georgian architecture is straight from a Jane Austen novel and its highlights are the iconic Royal Crescent and the Majestic Circus." Unfortunately, we weren't there for the spa.

The Roman Baths today are the site of extensive ruins and an interactive museum filled with treasures and visual snippets that take you back to Roman times and the lives of the Aqua Sulis people. We picked up an audio guide, and walked along ancient pavements as the Romans did 2000 years ago. We explored the chambers, historical changing rooms, and tepid plunge pools. Afterwards, in the Pump Room, we took a sip of the spa water which contains 43 minerals and is known for its curative purposes. It was a genuine walk through a very interesting time in England's history. We wandered the amazing ancient sidewalks until we found an appropriate pub with outdoor seating to have lunch, which was fish and chips of course! I also popped into a health food store that we were wandering by and picked up some activated charcoal capsules, which I had heard might be handy to have in Mexico, which was now only three days away! By mid-afternoon, we were back on the road for the last of our journey to London and we arrived just before dinner.

I had chosen a beautiful Marriott hotel in the London countryside, about 40 kilometres from central London, which was somewhat of a gamble distance-wise. We were able to all sleep in one room, breakfast was included, and it was situated on a scenic golf course. We arrived Friday afternoon and were only there for two nights, so how bad could it be? It was beautiful and in a gorgeous London countryside setting. We checked in, shuffled the third kid in through the side door, unpacked, and then headed back out in search of supper. A quick peruse of the hotel restaurant menu revealed that it was way out of our budget. There was no way we could eat there all weekend if we wanted to be able to fly onward to Mexico that Sunday. Our lovely countryside setting meant that heading out to find food wasn't going to come as easily as I had hoped. We finally landed on a corner fast food take-out joint that didn't look too busy and ended up eating fish and chips. Again! When in England…

To prepare for the next morning, I spent the evening mapping out our big day in London. Google maps was showing it was going to be about 40 km straight to central London, which would land us in the proximity of the Sandeman's walking tour that I had previously booked. It looked as though parking might be an issue, but I figured we would park where we could and just walk until we found the tour. Oddly though, Google predicted the drive was going to take about two hours and with nothing to compare it to, we chalked it up to an error and planned to be on the road by 8:00 am for our 10:00 am tour. If you've ever driven from rural London into the urban centre, you may have already identified our two big mistakes. First of all, parking isn't just *difficult*, it's a bloody nightmare if possible at all. Second, the two hours of travel the GPS had predicted was pretty accurate. London doesn't do highways, or freeways, or motorways, or interstates. London is made up of narrow, windy country roads with one billion traffic lights. I don't think it is an exaggeration to say that we stopped at more traffic lights on that trip into the city and back then we had on our entire trip up to this point. It was excruciatingly slow. After about twenty minutes we realized quickly that we were, in fact, not going to be exiting onto a faster road, but would be driving this very slow and painful road the entire way. Time was ticking, but luckily we somehow arrived in central London at the last possible moment, despite construction detours that came with every turn Google directed us to take. We tracked down a parking garage, threw our money at it, and ran like the wind to get to our meeting point. The large group was waiting for us in Covent Garden Plaza, where we signed in just as the rain started. Welcome to London!

The three-hour walking tour commenced with a bang, and highlighted Buckingham Palace, St. James Palace, the Nelson Column on Trafalgar Square, Big Ben, and ended at Westminster Abbey. The history and destinations were incredibly interesting, but it got progressively colder and windy, too. By the middle of the third hour, the boys were petering out and we were all hungry, so we darted off early to hunt for lunch. Central London is not the place to look for a quick family lunch place, so we ended up at TGI Friday's in desperation, eating a meal of expensive, franchise American food. It was delicious and familiar but was a little disappointing since food experiences are one of my favourite aspects of travel. We had covered the token fish and chips meal twice already but I would have loved nothing more than an afternoon tea experience with scones and clotted cream, or a bangers and mash meal with yorkshire pudding. But the reality presented a great reason to return someday, I guess. We didn't have much more on the itinerary for the day and after the long, arduous trip into the city we weren't very excited about driving further. Plus, it was still cold and raining so we decided that our day in London was a wrap.

I had made plans weeks earlier to meet up with Emily from Fiji, the girl that we had met in the pool and conquered the 'hike with Juta' with. She was as sweet as they come and had been texting me in anticipation of our arrival. We drove the two hours back to our hotel and Emily was waiting for us there. She insisted on buying us coffee and treats and we visited for hours. It was so fun to see her again, catch up, and hear the story of how the rest of her travels had unfolded. She was now back working in London at a hair salon and living with her parents. Fiji was just a memory, and she had dreams of traveling again soon. I was so thankful she had made the long trek out to our hotel in the country, and she apologized for the lack of freeways and shared in our misery of how awful it was to get into London from the outskirts.

Overall, London was just ok. I think the weather played a negative part in our day. Of course, the awful trek in and back didn't help, making us feel rushed and disjointed. In the end, the city probably didn't get a fair chance to woo us. All I remember clearly is a lot of sirens and low-flying helicopters that are apparently present whenever the Queen is home. London was extremely multi-cultural, dare I say much less 'English' than I was expecting. The areas that we drove through were mostly Arab and Indian communities with predominantly Muslim markets, shops, and restaurants and barely an English sign to be seen. Most neighbourhoods included a prominently placed, dirty, old, and unkempt mosque and it felt like a tour through a third-world, middle-eastern country. I know London has a lot more to offer, but we just didn't quite get the chance to see it. Maybe next time! Until then, our flight to the sun and sand awaited. We were cold and more than ready for Cancun, Mexico!

Travel Tip - Plan accommodation wisely. Stay where you want to explore, driving is chaotic, parking is a nightmare and London is an extremely busy city. Take in Sandeman's free walking tours whenever possible!

Blog Post: May 2017

We crash-landed in Cancun after the crazy amazing race through Europe tired, haggard, and jet lagged. We felt desperate for food and rest, which unfortunately wasn't going to make an appearance any time soon! The heat was there waiting for us along with Cancun's finest timeshare salespeople presenting themselves as tour guides (eye roll.) We spent way too much time listening to their pitches, wasting precious time trying to capitalize on getting something free. We did end up scoring a 'free' catamaran day tour to Isla Mujeres and a free breakfast which we used later in the week. They were not really free, of course, because they neglected to inform us about dock fees and taxes which of course are all in US dollars, adding 35% to the already ridiculously high prices.

Against my better judgement we hadn't arranged transportation to our bed and breakfast. It was Clint's suggestion, and a rookie mistake. We should have known better by this point. After an eleven-hour flight, time change, and with jet lag and no phone plan, we lugged our gear from city-bus to city-bus, to taxi, and to anyone that could possibly tell us where our stupid rental might be. As it turned out, it was a brand new listing in a gated subdivision. We were finally dropped off in front of the gates and spent an hour wandering from house to house, looking into people's windows and back yards, and banging on doors. The security guards found us, but didn't know which house it was either! We returned to the front gate and tried several phone numbers using the security guard's phone and finally made contact with someone who said they'd be there in ten minutes. We waited another hour and were joined in the meantime by a couple from France who spoke broken English and who were looking for the same place. Buddy finally showed up, let us in with barely an apology, and there we were. It was pouring rain and we ordered tacos to the house. We ate, and we crashed! Bienvenidos a Mexico!!

We spent two nights at the bed and breakfast before checking into our timeshare. They weren't our worst nights of the trip, but they were close. We walked a long way the next day to find food and water. At home, we found ourselves locked out of our bedroom while Clint madly searched for his bank card that, as it turned out, he had left in the bank machine. He took Rylan to go back for it while I spent an hour texting someone who I thought was the landlord, but who was actually someone of the same name and number located in Portugal who spoke no English. Good grief, I thought, can this weekend please just end? And, it did. In no time we were checking into our actual paradise on the beach.

The timeshare came with a pool, separate apartments, free laundry and an actual closet to hang our clothes in for only the third time in seven months. It was heavenly! We bought groceries, cooked, spent days doing almost nothing but snorkelling, reading, and playing beach volleyball and Bingo. I did do schoolwork with the boys in the mornings. I say morning loosely, as most days no one saw the light of day until at least 10:30 am. It felt like a real vacation without the cocktails and eating out! The kids loved it there, and we spent a few days touring around town in a rented car, joining locals at a city park for cheap food, and just exploring in general.

The next day we were scheduled to head off to Playa Del Carmen for a week, and then Tulum for ten days! The plan thus far was to spend half a day volunteering at an animal shelter, see some Mayan ruins, explore cenotes, more beaches, and hopefully snorkel with turtles! Mexico had been delightful so far and we were so happy to be there. We couldn't wait to see more!

CHAPTER 17

Mexico

Part One

Cancun, Mexico was an eleven-hour direct flight on Thomas Cook airlines from London. It seemed like a strange direct flight but as it turns out, the Brits love Mexico. It was a long eleven hours and we landed around dinner time, hungry, exhausted, and without a plan. In my defence, I had wanted a plan, but Clint hadn't felt we needed one, so this one was all on him! We had booked accommodations, but hadn't planned how to get there. If we had booked anywhere else in Cancun it wouldn't have been a problem, but I had booked a brand new listing on booking.com without a common name that the local taxis recognized, or a proper address. (I chose it because it was reasonably priced, had a kitchen, and looked like a comfortable fit for all five of us.) So, we took a taxi to a bus station close to the airport, climbed aboard, and were dropped off at a random neighbourhood that happened to be gated. No one on the security team spoke English, and they didn't appreciate us wandering around lost. Finally, one of them let us use his phone to call the only contact number I had been given. The man who answered said he'd be there shortly. We waited in the rain until he arrived an hour later, and when we were finally shown to our rooms, we discovered that we were sharing living quarters with a couple from France! Our stay was in the middle of nowhere, except that it was within walking distance to a small warehouse-style grocery store. We got locked out of our bedroom. The shower barely worked. It didn't take long for me to figure out why it was so cheap. We managed for two nights and then took a taxi to our first *real* destination, Raintree Vacation Villas on the Cancun strip, Club Regina.

Back home, Clint had befriended one of his Kamloops customers over years of service. Maureen was a sweet older lady who had frequently told him that she had a timeshare in Cancun that we were welcome to use, for free, if we ever went to Mexico! She was a retired school teacher and loved that we homeschooled our kids. She had met the boys a few times over the years when they would go to work with Clint, and our family had found a special place in her heart. So when the opportunity to go to Mexico presented itself, we checked in with her and she had been thrilled to help us out. Maureen had booked us for two weeks in two separate units, and the dates had been confirmed the day after our cruise ended. We had planned our European journey based on arriving in Mexico for our stay at the timeshare.

The last couple of days of travel had been pretty awful, and arriving at the villas felt like heaven on earth. The units were gorgeous and modern, and the beachfront complex was small, intimate, and easy to get around. There were plenty of activities both on and off the beach, and we had full kitchens and laundry. It was everything the doctor ordered and couldn't have come at a better time. We were tired of the cold and ready to relax in the sun after our amazing race through Europe and the UK. Our tentative plans after the stay at Maureen's included a week in Playa Del Carmen and then a week in Tulum, but by this point they weren't set in stone.

It was May; we had been on the road for six months. Clint and I weren't even close to feeling ready to return, but the boys were getting tired and missed their friends and the comforts of home. They started to push for a return plan. It would be my Grandma's 90th birthday party in Alberta during the first week of July, so we set that event on our calendar and began working towards it. We looked ahead, found the best flights back to Phoenix giving us about a month in Mexico, and began to discuss how we might wind up our adventure during the final weeks before returning to North America. But Clint and I wanted to stay in the present as much as possible, so we loaded up on groceries, scouted out some activities to do in the area, and decided to figure the rest out later.

We had visited Mexico many times over the years, but never on the eastern side, where Cancun is. The sand on our beach was gorgeous, white, and powdery. The water was warm and the waves were gentle enough that I could float my heart away. The boys played endless games of soccer on the beach, pretending Mexico vs. Canada, and pool-basketball too. In the evenings we played bingo and took long sunset walks, wondering how we would ever leave this paradise. We rented a car for a couple of days and explored some local Mayan ruins, found a mall and cooled off in the air-conditioning, and discovered a local park with food trucks and bands playing live music. The boys were still working on school for a couple of hours every day and I feverishly tried to plan out a long road trip home on our dwindling budget and the small amount of remaining credit card points. We only took two big excursions, the first being a cheap trip to Passion Island that we were sucked into signing up for through the timeshare. It included a catamaran tour, snorkelling, sports on the beach, lunch, and drinks, and was a fun day away from the resort. A few days later we took the ferry over to Isla Mujeres, where we had lunch at a cantina and rented a golf cart to explore around the island. We took some cool photos and returned later in the day, sunburned and tired.

About a month before we left the UK, Clint had heard from his longtime friend Cage to compare calendars. Cage and his wife Deb go to Belize for a month every spring, so they planned to fly into Cancun, stay a couple of nights to see us, and then drive to Belize from there. They booked two nights at the Club Med next door to us and flew in mid-afternoon one day, taking a quick nap before we met them at their beachfront hotel restaurant for dessert. It was so much fun to see them and reunite over drinks and dessert. Clint lit right up, like a kid in a candy store. Cage and he had been golf buddies for over ten years and they had booked a tee time for the next morning. We caught up on all the latest family news and shared about our adventures thus far. The budget came up in conversation as Clint and I had been hashing it out again lately, bothered by how much more we had spent than was planned for. We had been using the proceeds from the sale of our business to pay for the trip, and while there were still lots of money left we had a month of travel to go, and no idea of what we were going to do for work when we returned home. It was beginning to weigh heavily on Clint how over-budget we kept slipping. Cage brought some sound advice that helped tremendously. He reminded us that we could always go home and make another ten thousand dollars, but a trip like this was a once in a lifetime opportunity. He encouraged Clint to let it go and assured him that everything would be fine. I loved this advice since it happened to reflect my own mindset and I was so grateful for it! But sometimes it helps to hear it from someone else, so we transferred another ten thousand dollars to our spending account and planned the trip home.

Cage took the boys out spearfishing in the ocean the next day and they brought home their catch for dinner. That was a first in our family, and another wonderful memory! After a couple of days of catching up, we bid our friends farewell on their journey to Belize. If we had learned anything by this point, it was that all good things must come to an end. It was a sad goodbye.

Blog Post: June 2017

So a planned two weeks in Mexico turned into more than a month! Our paradise on the beach in Cancun came with the best showers, beds, and pillows of the entire trip, and by the time we checked out, the boys' homework was all caught up and everyone felt rested. We rented a car and headed for Playa del Carmen, ready for a change of scenery but wary as we had always come to be when arriving someplace unknown. Our accommodations were hard to find and did not have the waterpark, bike rentals, or tennis onsite, as was advertised on the booking.com listing. After shaking my finger at the French and Italian owners and attempting to communicate my displeasure in broken English and Spanish, they promised to correct their listing. (As of one month later, they had not.) This is Mexico—I guess they do things differently here.

We settled in as best we could. Our space had small beds and the hot water only dribbled out of a broken shower head, but overall the place was clean and cute. The Europeans really have a flare for design! We really couldn't complain though, since we had a kitchen, separate bedrooms, and a delicious cooked breakfast every morning for only $45.00 CAD per night. Waterpark, shmaterpark! We meandered around Playa del Carmen, locating the grocery store, finding bank machines, and updating our phones. We even set up a dentist appointment for Clint.

The afternoon we arrived, Braden stated, "So by tomorrow, we should feel comfortable around here, and know our way around too, just like we always do, right?" We had to laugh, as no truer statement had ever been made. Everything that is overwhelming and stressful and uncomfortable when arriving somewhere new becomes second nature in no time. Before we knew it, the boys were heading across the street to kick around a ball at the most beautiful neighbourhood soccer pitch. I got busy cooking, and Clint made his way to the dentist. Just like that, we were all settled in!

Playa, as the locals call it, provided a lovely local neighbourhood experience. We didn't have a big budget hotel, or fancy beach or pool, but we met people. We went to church, and made new friends, and spent lots of time just exploring the area. We even had the pleasure of volunteering at a local dog rescue one morning, cleaning up poop, and feeding and cuddling these sweet street dogs.

After a week, we felt excited to move a bit further south to Tulum. Clint had an old acquaintance from Kamloops that offered us his Airbnb for a great price, so we snapped it up and spent a week exploring the area. We climbed the ancient

Mayan Ruins of Coba, spent time at the beach, went to church, and swam in many local cenotes, which are sink holes that fill with cool, clean, and gloriously fresh groundwater. I kept the boys going with school, which was mostly math and quickly getting old, let me tell you! This teacher is tired and done.

It was in Tulum, that Braden declared that he finally started to realize that after this experience, he can see himself being less afraid of things once we get home. Travel has broken through some of his fearful nature. Later on, he mentioned that he also is beginning to feel that he doesn't need all the stuff we have in order to feel comfortable. Travel has helped him come to this. These sentiments are big victories for us as parents! After months of feeling like the kids didn't get it and sometimes even, in difficult moments, questioning whether we did the right thing by bringing them, these admissions were welcome relief and couldn't have come at a better time. Thank you God!

So all in all, Mexico in her convoluted glory of broken English, amazing food, corrupt government, fantastic music, terrible water, beautiful white sand beaches, and delightful hard working happy people, was a success! We spent our last three nights reuniting with our friends, sharing meals and talking until the wee hours of the morning. Another gift of travel has been people! We have met amazing people on this trip. We call them all our new friends for life. Only time will separate us from seeing them again. In the meantime, we orchestrated flights back to our van in Phoenix, and are beginning the mental preparation of arriving full-circle (literally!) on this dream trip around the world. It wasn't over yet, but the end was drawing near and we were grappling with thoughts about how to put our life back together, while simultaneously trying to push those thoughts away and remain focused on the present. We wanted to cram every last experience into our remaining time together. It felt a bit surreal to be heading toward home, but God knows all, and we always trust him with whatever is ahead. For the time being though, we had a road trip home to plan!

Mexico Part Two

We had no real idea of where we wanted to go from Cancun, but we rented a car and ended up in Playa del Carmen. I found another rental on booking. com that had big promises of all kinds of amenities that, unfortunately, it did not actually have. The modern, two-bedroom, ground-floor condo was located about five blocks from 5th Avenue, Playa's central location. It was comfortable, safe, and had air conditioning—all crucial basics. There was rarely any hot water though, and the broken shower head only dripped. The kitchen had no oven and was ill-equipped for even minimal cooking. The owners were two trendy men from Italy who spoke little to no English and were never any help whatsoever. However, I had booked a week prepaid, and even after getting nowhere with them I wasn't about to push it and risk a cancellation or refund. There was a highlight, and it was, again, the free breakfast.

Every morning at 10:00 am, we were served a hot Mexican breakfast on the upstairs rooftop veranda. The cook prepared eggs on toast layered with cheese, ham, and cilantro, topped with warmed black beans. It came with a side bowl of fresh papaya and bananas with sweetened vanilla yogurt. It was absolutely delicious. The boys discovered a fenced-in soccer pitch with nets a block away from our hotel, and were content to spend hours there. We weren't able to find much of a public beach anywhere close, so we spent most of our days not doing much. I worked on my blog, the boys finished what was left of their math, and Clint started looking for a dentist to see while we were in the area. He had been thinking of having an old problematic root canal looked at and the boys were due to get cleanings, but when his tooth broke off after he bit into a taco, it became a mini crisis. We rifled through reviews on an international dentist search site, settled on one, and booked appointments for the next day. The cleanings were non eventful, but Clint's x-ray showed that the root canal had been flawed and his tooth would need major repair. We weren't prepared to do the work at the time, so they decided to pull it. He booked a follow up appointment for the next week, took pain meds in the meantime, and we prayed the pain and irritation wouldn't get worse.

After a ton of research I found a local, English-speaking, non-denominational church service. It had been weeks since we had been to church and I was eager to return, hoping to meet some people from the area, and make an acquaintance or two or at a minimum. We attended the first Sunday we were in town. It was a small service with some familiar songs and a great message from the pastor, who was Mexican but who had lived in the States for years. He had returned to Playa Del Carmen a few years earlier with his American family to lead the church. Everyone we met was warm and welcoming, and made a point to shake our hands and listen to our story. One couple in particular took a real interest in our adventure. Ken and Leticia were an American couple with three kids who had sold everything and moved to live in this little paradise. After a while, they started to dream of gutting and transforming an old school bus to travel across the United States in. They invited us to join them for a trip to the mall after church. We met at the food court and after lunch the boys went to see a matinee movie with their two daughters. Ken and Leticia were so excited for us and our journey and couldn't hear enough about it. They invited us to their home for coffee when we were done at the mall, where we talked some more about our experience and encouraged them in their pursuit of their travel dream. We would be leaving the next day to spend a week in Tulum, so we made plans to meet again to spend more time together later in the week.

I had been given a recommendation for a local animal rescue centre that we could volunteer at. I contacted the owner over Facebook and made arrangements to meet at a local coffee shop, making our way from there into the jungle to the Riviera Rescue. To describe the place as ramshackle would be an understatement, but the owners definitely made an honest go of trying to keep stray dogs off the street and take care of the ones that they could. In our brief chat they explained that they had been inspired to start the project after seeing all the stray dogs during their many trips to Mexico. They made it work relying mostly on word of mouth among travellers for assistance running the place. They put us to work cleaning up dog poop, changing water dishes, raking up rocks and debris from the caged areas, and cuddling whatever doggies we felt like while we worked. The boys were in heaven, and in no time were playing with and chasing a couple mutts that were particularly attracted to them. We made a promise to get Braden a dog when we got home. He is the family member that is especially drawn to animals and it was refreshing to see him light up in their presence.

It was nice to be able to give back, if even for a short while. We were nearing the end of our adventure and I had now exhausted any and all leads and/or dreams I had of being able to be of service as a family. It just hadn't worked out as I had hoped it would. There were a long list of reasons why but it was still disappointing.

Our week in Playa del Carmen was coming to an end. Clint remembered he had another Kamloops business contact who owned properties in Tulum and Belize, so he called him up and secured a rental for the next week in Tulum. It was a higher-end, comfortable, two-bedroom condo in an apartment complex with a pool. It was also within walking distance to town. We loaded up on groceries for the week and scouted out Trip Advisor and my Facebook traveling families group for things to do in the area.

The beach in Tulum was postcard-worthy and closely rivalled some of our favourites from Australia. We found an old sandy road that led to a public beach parking lot which was easily accessible and we spent many afternoons hanging out there. The boys joined in a group volleyball game and frolicked in the waves while Clint and I relaxed on the soft white sand, enjoying every moment of the beautiful, hot sunshine that we could.

The two main recommendations we had gotten were to climb the Coba Ruins and visit the local cenotes. It was about an hour's drive to Coba, so we packed a lunch and headed out early one morning in an attempt to get there before the bus loads of tourists arrived. Coba dates back to around 750 BC and is believed to have had over 50,000 inhabitants during its time. The total site spans about 50 kilometres, but we only covered a 4 to 5 kilometre area during our visit. We rented bikes and explored this jewel in the Mexican jungle for hours. It is 120 steps to the top of the main temple, Nohoch Muul, which is 138 feet high. I made it about 10 steps before my slippery, sweaty, and basically dangerous flip flops stopped me. Carson had no interest in going up, but the other three made it all the way to the top, where they took another trip-highlight selfie with the most spectacular view as a reward. From there, we followed Google maps to Choo-Ha Cenotes, a series of three cenotes in the same area. We changed into our suits and descended the narrow, rickety, wooden staircase into what felt like the centre of the earth for a relaxing and refreshing dip in its cool, crystal-clear blue waters, which was a welcome relief from the sweltering humidity. These cenotes were off the main tourist path, lesser known and rarely mentioned in traveling circles. We had them all to ourselves. The second cenote had man-made 5- and 10-meter high platforms jetting out from the rock walls, from which the boys honed their cliff jumping and diving skills while I floated nearby in terror, just praying we survived this little foray into the centre of the earth. I had long since given up any hope of restraining them, especially when it came to jumping and flipping off of any high surface. Thank God they tended to be cautious in life, so we reminded them to check depth first, and let them at it. We made it home for dinner and were exhausted and ready to go to bed early.

We ventured out to several more cenotes over the week in Tulum, some basic and some with elaborate swings and zip lines. Visiting these groundwater-filled sinkholes was an inexpensive activity and always a fantastic reprieve from the afternoon heat.

Another place off the beaten path that had come highly recommended was Valladolid, a city of about 50,000 founded in 1543, located in the eastern part of Yucatan. Valladolid was a great place to explore the history and culture of the Yucatan Peninsula. It has colonial-era churches and architecture, as well as natural attractions like cenotes, and one notable site is the Convent of San Bernardino de Siena. Yucatan is known for its Longaniza which is a pork-based salami served with traditional condiments. Other treats include locally made traditional candies and ice cream made out of coconut, corn, and honey. We wandered the plaza and historic cobblestone streets surrounded by shops and restaurants. By mid afternoon, we were sweaty and dying of heat and could not have been more excited to stumble upon Cenote Zaci, located right in the heart of the city. The cenote was hidden from view from the parking lot, but we followed signs down a long, steep, and wet staircase to find a landscaped, freshwater, underground sinkhole. It was grander than any that we had seen so far and we were enamoured by the beauty as the sun streaked in through the long mosses and plant life dangling from above. Photos could never do it justice. I stumbled on the last step and slid hard into the crushed rock of the walkway and almost bailed over the ledge into the water. It probably looked like Fail Army material in the moment, but I was overwhelmed with screeching pain and looked down to see my knee and toe completely carved open and bleeding, and failed to find the humour. I staggered over to the makeshift area where my family had strewn their towels and the rest of our belongings. My day in the water ended before it even began, but I occupied myself by taking videos of the boys climbing the slippery wet rock to the highest ledges they could reach. They impressed bystanders below barrelling into the water with their backflip 360s and gainers. Although I was still in a lot of pain, the experience was breathtaking and magical.

The last place on my Tulum bucket list was a well-known tourist trap for seeing and swimming with turtles. I knew it would be busy and had heard through my online groups that it was quite the political production to get to now that the government had intervened, but I wanted one last special activity to do, and we hadn't snorkelled much since Australia. The locals apparently had been complaining for years that the tourists were damaging the coral and disrupting the ecosystem of the turtles and sea life, so the government installed "water cops" and parking lot attendants to attempt to deter all of the traffic. The discrepancy was that some felt the water cops were self appointed and it was a money grab, and not a government initiative at all. We arrived reasonably early and were directed to pre-arranged parking spots where they charged $10 US dollars just to park for the day—an annoying start. The beach was already packed and the swimming area was roped off. It was expected that you rent their gear and pay a fee to swim out past the rope, this was what appeared to be the gimmick of the operation. The advice I had been given was to just ignore it and do as we chose, so that's what we did. All of us with the exception of Clint are strong swimmers so we headed out without life jackets and a guide. Clint stayed back at the beach, since he was uncomfortable with currents and was starting to disdain salt water. We were about 100 feet out when I heard a shrieking whistle from behind. A large and aggressive Mexican was swimming towards us and running out of breath, yelling that we couldn't go any further without a permit. I ignored him and continued on since I had been warned about this gimmick. He got closer and began threatening to physically restrain us if we didn't listen, and I was unsure whether or not he meant it. Another couple swam up beside us and we conversed quickly, trying to determine whether he was police or was this a joke. We all decided after enough harassment that it wasn't worth it. I'd lost the excitement of being there anyway. Luckily, we did happen to be passed by an enormous turtle not far beneath the surface of the water, so we snapped a few photos with our underwater camera and headed back to the beach. We told Clint about our big adventure with the crazy Mexican ocean cop and another couple, overhearing my story, said as long as we swam outside of the swimming ropes there was nothing they could do to stop us.

Two of the boys were done (and likely traumatized) but Carson and I were ready to try again. Against my better judgement, we swam out without life jackets and got extremely distracted by the sea life just below the surface. Before long, I realized we were quite far from land and told Carson we'd better head back before the water got too deep. We weren't seeing anything very exciting anyway, and I was still feeling generally disappointed. I started to kick and push the water beneath me, but the current was strong and whenever I lifted my head it seemed that we hadn't moved. We were too far out to yell for help and I was suddenly aware that this was unsafe. The harder I tried to swim in, the more I felt like I wasn't moving. Carson seemed okay just ahead of me, but I didn't want to ask him or let him know I was starting to panic, feeling upset with myself for being careless. I was also getting extremely tired. My arms and legs were exhausted and it still didn't feel like we were making progress. My heart was pounding out of my chest and I prayed silently to God to help us get back to shore. I was terrified, until suddenly I wasn't. In the midst of panic my mind cleared and I was overcome with determination NOT to drown out here, meters from the shore. I put my head in the water with my mask on and pushed and kicked for dear life. Remarkably, this time I noticed the ocean floor moving beneath me, confirming that we were making progress even though it still didn't seem that way whenever I raised my head. So I kept my head down, pushed and paddled my feet, and before long could feel the glorious touch of sand from the ocean floor beneath with the tips of my toes. We were still far out, but at least we would be able to stand on the bottom soon. I could not have been more thankful when we finally reached shore. As I told my family my terrifying tale of almost drowning, Carson laughed and said he had been totally fine and had no idea I was having a full blown panic attack behind him. Lesson learned!

We met up with Ken and Leticia one last time in Puerto Morelos for ice cream cones and a lovely walk around the quaint beachside town. We took in one last local church service, at an outdoor English-speaking Baptist church that seemed mainly made up of expats and tourists, in a seedy back alley of Tulum. We met a few more people, and shook a few more hands as our memorable time in Tulum started to wind down. We still had three nights before our flight to Phoenix, where our round the world adventure would end.

We had originally planned a weekend with Ken and Leticia in Campeche, Mexico where their son, whom we had not yet met, was in boarding school. Unfortunately, they had to change plans at the last moment, so we decided to book two nights back in Playa del Carmen where we could visit with them some more and meet some of their other local American friends. We shared a potluck dinner with them all, trading stories and laughing. I went home that night with an arm's-length piece of aloe vera for my leg. When you ask a friend in Mexico for aloe vera, you don't get a little snip of their house plant like you do in Canada, you get a whole branch hacked off their backyard aloe tree! We returned to the church once more before we left, and had a meal afterward with a collection of people from the congregation at a delicious local brunch place. Playa del Carmen was starting to feel like home just as we prepared to leave. We spent one last night in Cancun, contacting my cousin Jessica who would meet us at the airport in Phoenix, and printed our boarding passes. One magical and memorable month in Mexico came to an end. The boys were eager to start the trek home but I sat with my grief, knowing it would all soon be just a memory.

Travel Tip - Get away from the tourist trap areas in Mexico and explore like a local. Use Facebook groups and Trip Advisor for advice and don't be afraid to rent a car and explore. We were only mildly worried about getting stopped by crooked police, so I kept all of the cash on me or hidden in the car so Clint wouldn't have a wallet full in the event we did. We had no problems.

Blog Post: June 2017

We have quite literally come full circle, around the world, back to where we started. Phoenix was a balmy and delightful 42 degrees when we landed. Yes, I said balmy and delightful. We love the heat but after soaking in our own sweat day and night for eight months, a dry 42 came as a welcome relief, even at the expense of chapped lips, parched skin, and the occasional bloody nose! We had barely made it inside my cousin's house before the kids descended on our van like it was a long-lost family member. I truthfully could barely remember what she looked like inside and was pleasantly surprised. We have a really nice van! After driving thousands of kilometres all over the world in rented five-seater mini cars, the space and comfort felt like heaven. We cuddled our own blankets and pillows and the boys reunited with their long lost Playstation 4. Carson laced up his skates and took some shots with his beloved and badly missed hockey stick. We had a great couple of days in Phoenix, cleaning and reorganizing, repacking, and getting ready to hit the road. This road trip comes with mixed emotions, because eight months ago it was supposed to be a three-month road trip up through the east coast of the US and Canada before heading west to home. That alone was something of a dream trip in itself.

As our trip progressed, we have had to shorten this final journey and nix certain things. As of right now, we are left with hitting New Mexico and then traveling north through Colorado, Wyoming and Montana and then home, over the course of a month. I grapple with wavering feelings; feeling blessed and content with what we have been able to do, and sad about the many things that have been missed out on along the way. This was one casualty, and there had been many more. When cleaning the van I found the stack of brochures and travel books for the eastern side of our continent that I had saved under my seat in anticipation; all garbage now. It's hard, to be honest, sharing about the many times I have shed tears over what has felt like the death of my full dream, when all everyone sees is us gallivanting around the world doing things most people would never do in their lifetime. I get it. I really do and I'm not complaining. My heart is full, but I still feel sad about the things I wish we could have done. We gave up a good life for the sake of following this dream of mine that has been recreated many times along the way. Mostly I'm terrified that we will get home and feel stuck again in no time. Tied down to a life not of our choosing, exactly, but based on our kids' needs and desires, unable to do the things we missed out on and are left still wanting to do. Clint and I are both nervous right now.

So off we go, our van loaded to the hilt! Backpacking was so much easier, believe it or not. Oh my word, the stuff in here that we have packed up! We hit Tucson first, checking into our less than desirable but cheap roadside motel for two nights. There's no better way to ditch the crappy hotel blues than to hit the mall and shop till we drop. In no time, everyone had scrapped their crusty, worn, and tired clothes and were sporting new shirts and shorts. Clint even scored himself a whole new set of golf clubs. We acted like kids in a candy store! We ate pancakes at IHOP and drank cold tap water—it's been awhile. Welcome home!

The thing about travel is that it is very hard to know what is ahead, even in a familiar country such as the US. It is difficult to plan where to stop, how long to stay, where to book. Will we like it? Will we not? Will we wish we had stayed longer or wished we could leave but can't? All the research and advice in the world won't necessarily tell you what works for your family. As we pulled into Las Cruces, New Mexico for what was supposed to be two nights, I could tell in a moment that we would want to stay longer. What I expected was a smallish, old, run-down but historically unique city with a Mexican aesthetic, a few good museums, and maybe a good hike. To our surprise, Las Cruces was nothing but. The city sprawled far and wide, with a clean, Mexico-but-modern vibe. We found malls, JCPenney, blue skies, and an upgraded studio room with a kitchen and two queen beds in each of two bedrooms. We were sold! I hit the front desk looking to extend our stay on points to five nights (the fifth night is always free, so, no brainer.) Even the kids were chirping from the back of the van, "Can we stay here longer?" We were able to work it out and we stayed for five nights. Clint found himself golf courses that only charge $20 per round, and I found myself a Whole Foods-style health food store and went a little crazy reuniting with kombucha, good face cream, and organic mangos. The sweet life of travel; you never know where it will take you! We were able to relax in the heat by a lovely pool and had plenty of time to keep plugging away at that dang math. Our very comfortable accommodation provided us each with some space and comforts that reminded us of home. The museums were free, and there was lots to see and do. Braden turned fourteen during our stay and we planned a day trip to El Paso, Texas for waterslides and outlet shopping. This road trip got off to a good start!

CHAPTER 18

USA

Our original itinerary had included a visit, near the end of the trip, to Haiti. Our besties had moved there with their family just months before we had started our journey, so we were due for a visit. Scott and Tanya had adopted their two daughters, Ellie and Addie, from Haiti several years ago and had visited the country many times over the years, but more recently felt God's call to serve there on a permanent basis. They had sold their home in Kelowna, BC the summer of 2016 and had moved to Haiti to help with the operation of a children's home run by a Christian organization.

Scott went to work immediately, cleaning the property up, making it more efficient, and working on general maintenance and construction projects that had long been needed. The orphanage was located near one of the biggest hospitals in Haiti which predominantly employed expat doctors. Tanya recognized the need for a reprieve for the doctors, so she went to work building a coffee and smoothie café named TiKokoye that served sandwiches and snacks, offered massages and pedicures, and sold the work of local crafters and artisans. She employed a full staff of local Haitian women and although it had been a painstaking process to get the business up and running, it was now thriving and we could not wait to go and see the fruits of their labour.

Unfortunately, life had other plans. While we were still at Club Regina in Cancun and I was researching flights back to the US from Mexico,

I had attempted to arrange any combination of reasonable flights that might get us to Haiti first, and then to the US. We were still flexible in terms of time, but our budget was definitely running low. I spent hours comparing destinations, one way car rentals, and budget flights in and out of Haiti, but just could not make it work. We'd hoped to stay with them as guests, but the children's home had a policy of charging $25 US per person, per day, which worked out to $2,500 CAD for the two weeks that we had wanted to stay. Additionally, the flights were thousands of dollars more than we expected and had frustrating connections. Eventually, we had to make the dreaded decision not to go, and phone our friends in disappointment that it wasn't going to happen. We were all devastated. I am unsure that we made the right decision. Cage's words echoed in my mind; you can make another $5,000 anytime! I knew this was a once in a lifetime chance to have both of our families all together in Haiti. I cried over the decision, and somehow proceeded to muster together a plan to get us back to the States.

Flights back to Phoenix weren't overly expensive but they were coming in much higher than expected, considering they were one way and a relatively short distance. So I changed the search to fly to Las Vegas instead and then just rent a car to drive to Phoenix. Those flights were much cheaper but I noticed immediately that they included a Phoenix connection. I was so puzzled about why these flights were cheaper until I did a little research and discovered 'throw away flights'. Basically, flights into major US hubs (Phoenix is one) are priced much higher, regardless of the distance or whether or not it is a direct flight. There are even websites that sell throw away flights. It is something of a dirty travel secret, but people do it all the time! The only gamble is that travellers who do it often risk being flagged by the airlines themselves, and blocked from buying tickets in the future. The flights I found to Vegas were with an airline we had never flown with before nor had plans to fly with again, so I felt confidant we wouldn't have any problems. The only other major concern was making sure our baggage didn't get sent on ahead to Vegas when we got off in Phoenix. When we'd flown to Fiji I'd learned that most airlines allowed you to book a 'multi-city' ticket, and for the same price the stopover was free. So I did just that. I booked our super cheap one-way flights to Phoenix for June 11th, with the connection to Vegas for the following day, and we were golden! We landed in Phoenix that afternoon, picked up our luggage and away we went! Hopefully someone enjoyed having those five wide open seats to Vegas to themselves the next day!

My cousin Jessica was faithfully waiting for us at the Phoenix airport with our van. We were so excited to see our van after all those months. It's a nice van, and brought some home-comfort though we wouldn't be home for weeks yet. We grabbed dinner for all of us on the way back to her house and spent the next couple of days reuniting with her and her lovely family. What a wonderful and welcoming return to North America. We sketched out another basic road trip itinerary to get home, still based on being present for my Grandma's birthday party. The plan was to head south to Tucson, then over to Las Cruces and Albuquerque, New Mexico, before turning north to Colorado, Utah, Wyoming, Montana, and then home. We had roughly planned about three weeks to do it all, allowing two to three nights in each place and hopefully one longer stop. Our house was still rented out, but we wanted to make a pit stop in Kamloops for a few nights before heading to Alberta, to see friends, check in on our house, and deal with some paperwork and mail. By this point, we had been out of the country for seven months.

We spent the first two nights at a dodgy roadside motel in Tucson, Arizona—the kind where you hope the deadbolt works well. There wasn't much happening in Tucson, especially for anyone on a budget. We basically weren't feeling it, so we decided to move on. The one thing we did discover in Tucson was the mall! We had forgotten how exciting it was to shop, and to shop for cheap! So we hit up JC Penny and bought a ton of new clothes, which by now were badly needed. All of our shoes were worn almost through. The boys had outgrown everything, so we got them new shirts and shorts. I bought a second hand bag, and Clint was in the market for some new golf clubs and found a great deal at a discount golf warehouse.

It was only a four-hour drive to Las Cruces, New Mexico and, though I'm not sure why we chose this little gem, the city was a beauty to drive into, our hotel was great with two bedrooms and a kitchen, the golf was cheap, and we definitely wanted to stay longer. So I bumped our two nights up to five and we were set.

Las Cruces was scorching hot but beautiful. I snuck away for a few hours to hit the Old Navy and a Whole Foods store, Clint hit the links daily and the boys were happy to be settled for a couple of days. Our first big outing was a day trip down to El Paso, Texas where we had heard there was a Wet 'n' Wild waterpark. Carson wasn't into it, so Clint dropped the rest of us off and took him golfing for the afternoon. I brought my book and enjoyed some peace and quiet while Braden and Rylan hit the waterpark with their underwater camera for some amazing vlog footage. They had been faithfully recording every day for their cute personal project, *Desmar Vlogs*. Rylan generally did the filming, while Braden spent hours every night editing and creating music and background for all of their videos. It was quite a labour of love and it was so satisfying as a parent to see them work so hard on something and learn it all on their own. I always posted their vlogs to my social media feeds so our family and friends could get a (shaky) live-action update of our adventures.

Braden turned fourteen the week that we were in Las Cruces, and his special birthday dinner was at our favourite US fast food place, Chick-Fil-A. For dessert we stopped for my favourite USA treat, Caliche's Frozen Custard. I don't know why we don't have frozen custard in Canada, so anytime I can find it, I get excited. The next day we planned to drive out to White Sands National Park to see the sand dunes, but at the last minute someone suggested that we go late in the day when the temperatures cooled, there would be fewer people, and we could catch an amazing sunset. We loved the idea, so headed out at around 4:00 pm. We stopped at the Visitor Centre, rented discs for the boys to slide down the dunes with, and got some information on where to drive and where not to as we headed into the park. Before long, we crossed an old cattle guard into a white winter wonderland of sand. White Sands is 710 square kilometres of white gypsum sand crystals. According to the info centre, this gypsum dune field is the largest of its kind on Earth. The depth of the sand across the entire field is about 30 feet deep, while the tallest dunes are about 60 feet. The dunes were said to be formed 7 - 10 thousand years ago from exposed selenite crystals that gradually eroded into gypsum grains, and were transported eastward by prevailing winds. Fossilized footprints of Columbian mammoths, ground sloths, ancient camels, dire wolves, American lions and sabre-toothed cats have been uncovered in and around the western section of the park. To say it was magical and breathtaking is a drastic understatement.

The dunes were about a mile in from the visitor centre. There were picnic tables, backcountry camping spots, and nine miles of marked trails. White Sands attracts over half a million visitors every year and though there are several ranger guided tours and hikes, we were quite happy to see it all on our own. We parked at the base of the first dune and the boys grabbed their sleds and ran for the top. They slipped and slid and rolled around, top to bottom, over and over again. I grabbed our picnic blanket and snacks while Clint wrestled with the boys and chased them back and forth. The other advantage to coming later in the day is the sand was cooled off enough to walk on with bare feet. It was soft and feather light and felt like powder on the skin. The sunset was gorgeous and completely worth waiting for. It melted down behind the rolling hills of sand, leaving a pink trace and golden glow in its wake. We posed for photos, took sand stunting videos for the boys' vlog and drove back to our home-away-from-home for a moonlight swim in the pool.

From Las Cruces we drove six hours north to Albuquerque where we spent two nights, then continued to Montrose, Colorado for two more. While staying in Montrose, we took a day trip out to the Black Canyon of the Gunnison National Park. This stop was a suggestion from my dad, so we incorporated a small detour into our route to be able to see it. Black Canyon, like the Grand Canyon, has two primary entrances, the south rim and the north rim. The park contains twelve miles of the forty-eight-mile long Gunnison River. The canyon's name owes itself to the fact that parts of the gorge only receive half an hour of sunlight each day. After spending an afternoon there we would agree with this description from the book, *Images of America: The Black Canyon*: "Several canyons of the American West are longer and some are deeper, but none combines the depth, sheerness, narrowness, darkness and dread of the Black Canyon." We took the opportunity whenever possible to pull over and take small walks, pose for photos over the black edges, and the boys were entertained by their yells into the canyon echoing back at us. We ate our picnic lunch at the day use area and continued our drive along the narrow windy black cliff faces and arrived back in Montrose by dinnertime.

After that, we continued north, stopping in Grand Junction for two nights and followed that up with the longest leg of the drive yet—ten hours to Vernal, Utah, where we stayed for another five nights. Thus far, we hadn't paid for a single hotel room on this road trip home; our credit card points had been covering it. But we were now stretching the last points as far as they would go. We had booked five nights in a tiny room with two queen beds at The Town and Country Inn and Suites. The kitchen was ill-equipped and one kid had to sleep on the floor. It looked like it was going to be a long five nights, not to mention that when first driving through, Vernal seemed a sleepy, old, and small town without much to offer but Dinosaur Monument, which wouldn't take more than an afternoon. We got busy trying to figure out how we were going to kill five days. We loaded up on groceries, browsed a JC Penney, Clint golfed, and we found a church to attend on Sunday. It was a small, family church and they welcomed us with open arms. They handed out hand-decorated sugar cookies to their guests as a welcome gesture and we had the privilege of hearing some mission trip testimonies.

After a few nights in Vernal, things started to go south with me emotionally. I don't remember specifically what triggered it, but it was likely money again, and our close quarters were getting under my skin. It felt unfair that Clint was getting a reprieve golfing every day, and that the boys had video games to take their mind off things. In hindsight, I should have taken a couple of quiet afternoons to myself and found a library or coffee shop to enjoy. But instead, Clint and I had a gigantic blowout and I had a meltdown, which resulted in me moving to the hotel next door for the night. As Carson remembers it, *Vernal is where my parents separated for a night.* We didn't separate. Clearly he's never seen Friends; *we were on a break!* And a nice break it was, though it left me feeling terrible and full of guilt. As usual, I waited too long to voice my struggles and the flood gates opened wide. I think I was starting to let the sadness of getting closer to home creep in, coupled with feeling cramped and increasingly tapped financially. We were getting questions and pressure from home, anticipating our arrival back and the kids were more and more excited every day to get there. I was nowhere near done. We had nowhere to fight it out, no privacy whatsoever and I was in a small space with too many people but had never felt so lonely in my feelings. I needed some space and a change of scenery.

We continued to avoid conversations about home, but the subject was definitely on all our minds. I dreaded every aspect of it. Clint was excited to see family and friends but otherwise not looking forward to reality. The boys simply could not get back fast enough. They couldn't wait for their sports and friends, our home and their beds, Tim Hortons, the list went on and on. Back in Mexico, Clint and I had had a good talk one day while out floating in the ocean. I asked him if faced with the choice to go anywhere and do anything without money as an object, would he go home? The answer was a resounding no for both of us. Unfortunately—we agreed—this next season of life had to be about the boys and their lives and dreams, not ours. We couldn't put a finger on what exactly we would have chosen to do anyway, but maybe that's because it wasn't a dream open for discussion. For now, it would have to just stay a dream.

It was a sad conversation, and reality check for me, to voice aloud what I knew; it was too late in their childhoods to tote them off somewhere exotic again anytime soon, for as long as we had just done. Carson in particular had big hockey dreams and it was going to be a miracle if this trip didn't already mess that future up for him. He was also still chatting online with the girl he had been talking to since we left. We asked him repeatedly if his friendship with her was changing status. He always said no, my instinct knew better. And, while Clint had had a first-hand taste of the travel life, I feared his desire for more would be forgotten and left behind in the chase for another business and with the comfort of home and friends. I didn't have a clue how I was going to return and begin to live that old life all over again. But I knew I wasn't really being given the choice.

In the morning I returned to our cramped hotel room with my tail between my legs and we packed a lunch for our date with the dinosaurs. Dinosaur National Monument contains over eight-hundred paleontological sites and has fossils of all the major dinosaurs including Allosaurus and Abydosaurus, of which they have a skull, lower jaw and the first four neck vertebrae. The area around the quarry was declared a National Monument in 1915. The 'Wall of Bones,' located in the Dinosaur Quarry building, consists of a steeply-tilted rock layer which contains hundreds of dinosaur fossils. It was the closest any of us had ever been to walking with the dinosaurs, and even though the boys tended to not appreciate science or history, this place felt like a special place in the world to all of us.

We were now all done with Vernal, Utah and excited to see where the rest of this long road home would take us. Next stop, Lava Hot Springs.

CHAPTER 19

Homeward Bound

From Utah we headed north, taking a small scenic stop at Soda Springs, Idaho to watch a geyser of underground carbonated water that is let loose every hour on the hour as a tourist attraction. In 1934 'town fathers' were looking for hot water for a bathing attraction and instead drilled into a chamber of highly pressurized carbon dioxide gas and cold water. After running for weeks and flooding the downtown area, the geyser was capped and is manually released now. We arrived right on time and watched in awe from the viewing platforms as it broke forth from the ground and shot straight up into the sky. From there we continued on to our next destination, Lava Hot Springs, Idaho.

We arrived on a hot day, too early to check in to our apartment, so we grabbed lunch and paid to enter the Lava Hot Springs' waterslide and pool area. I perched myself under a tree with my book for the day while the boys and Clint hit the waterslides and diving platforms. Later that evening, after baking some box brownies and getting another road trip cooler packed, Clint and I snuck off to the actual hot springs. Bubbling out of natural underground springs, the hot water is rich with minerals but has no sulphur odour, which is a typical characteristic of hot springs. The five outdoor gravel and rock pools range in temperature from 102 to 112 degrees F and were surrounded in white glowing twinkle lights. It was a magical, romantic way to end the day.

The next day we took a long but scenic trip through Red Canyon National Forest and Jackson Hole Wyoming, en-route to Yellowstone National Park. We tried not to stop too many times, as nothing is worse than arriving late, cranky, and hungry to a foreign city, but it was hard not to since every site was more astounding and inspiring than the last. We had also planned the day so that our last tourist stop would be Yellowstone Park, and our stop for the night in Bozeman, Montana was another hour of driving beyond that. So we were watching the time to ensure we would see Yellowstone properly.

We made it to Yellowstone a few hours before dark, found a picnic table for a late lunch and read over the history of the park to the kids. Yellowstone National Park is widely held to be the first national park in the world. It's known for its wildlife and many geothermal features, especially the Old Faithful Geyser, which we had the pleasure of witnessing. It spans an area of almost 9,000 square kilometres and is composed of beautiful green-blue lakes, canyons, rivers, and mountain ranges. Half of the world's geysers and hydrothermal features are located in Yellowstone. We journeyed through the park, stopping for photos and short scenic walks out to the smaller geysers and other unique vantage points. By mid-afternoon I was getting a migraine, the boys were done exploring, and it began to rain, so we hit the highway to Bozeman. We found our Airbnb, unpacked, and were excited to eat at Olive Garden for the first time in almost a year.

At the restaurant, our waiter welcomed us to Montana and suggested that we go to Bozeman Hot Springs, their premiere tourist attraction. He said they had ten outdoor pools of varying temperatures in a naturesque setting, with twinkle lights. If there was anything I ever looked forward to on a road trip, it was finding the hot tub or spa at whatever hotel we stayed at, as soon we arrived. I absolutely lived for hot water and this sounded like exactly what the doctor ordered. Unfortunately the medication for my headache was making me sleepy already. As much as I would have loved to go and check it out, I could barely keep my eyes open at the table. Clint was ready to just head home and watch some TV for the night, too. So we unanimously passed on the suggestion and I hit the hay the moment we returned and rested up for one of our longest journeys yet. We only had two days left before we would cross into Canada and planned to take a small detour on the Going-to-the-Sun Road through Glacier National

Park. It would be another long day on the road, but it was one of the parks we were the most excited about seeing.

We woke up bright and early for our big day ahead, threw together some breakfast, packed lunch for the park, and checked out of our Airbnb. Interestingly enough, this was our one and only Airbnb of the trip. I had used it repeatedly as a search for affordable accommodations but it always, without fail, came out higher priced than anything else by the time we added fees and cleaning and admin costs. The single reason we used it this time was I had been saving a $50 off coupon code for a while now and thought it was time to finally cash it in and the place suited our needs great. We drove five hours to Logan Pass Visitor Centre which is the welcome stop at the eastern entrance of the park. They gave us the tour route and some information about scenic points, we paid our fee and were on our way. Our first experience of Glacier National Park was seeing the fleet of restored 1930's 'red jammers' produced by the historic White Motor Company. The classic vehicles are available for large group tours on all the main roads of the park. We spotted them everywhere! The park encompasses over one million acres and includes parts of two mountain ranges, over 130 named lakes, more than 1,000 different species of plants, and hundreds of species of animals. The vast and pristine ecosystem of the park is the centrepiece of what has been referred to as "The Crown of the Continent Biosphere Reserve," a region of protected land encompassing 16,000 acres. Another unique and magical feature of this amazing destination is the two hundred waterfalls scattered throughout the park. Many flow over and alongside the road and we were in awe to drive right through a couple of them. The highlight was following the scenic Going-to-the-Sun Road that was completed in 1932. It is 50 miles long, and the only road that traverses the park, crossing the Continental Divide through Logan Pass at an elevation of 6,646 feet, which is the highest point on the road. The genius behind getting this road built, and so many years ago, is nothing short of an architectural marvel.

The park was fairly busy that day, so we were continually at the mercy of the car ahead as there was no passing allowed. Clint and I argued about where to stop to eat our lunch. I was hoping to find a decent pull-out where we could throw a blanket on the ground and explore for a while. He wanted to pull over at the height of it, happy to eat in the van as long as we had the views. I happened to win this time, and although we couldn't find an area designated for picnics, we did find a parking lot next to a river that had some rapids and rocks the boys could climb and explore. It was a gorgeous spot and ending up being a great find, since we had been in the van for hours. We had another couple of hours until we would arrive at Whitefish, Montana, where we had booked the last night we could on credit card points. It was a reminder of how far we had travelled, and how far the points had lasted us. I could have never known all those years ago when I signed up for that credit card, that it would take us around the world and back again on free points. It ended up being the absolute wisest decision we made in preparation for our trip. Our last stretch before crossing into Canada, where we planned to spend the night in Creston, BC, was an uneventful four hours, until we had a little run in with Bambi. It was getting to that point in a long drive when you are physically and emotionally done, but still have a ways to go. We had stopped for some 'pick-me-up' snacks and Clint made the mistake of getting a Starbucks frappucino. If you've never seen Clint get hyper on caffeine and sugar, you've missed out in life. About 45 minutes later he was jacked, the music was cranked, and the pedal was getting pushed. I moved to the back because I could tell we were in for a fight, letting Braden move up to my seat. Not five minutes later, I heard Braden yell "Dad!" The van swerved, there was a large thump, and I sat up just fast enough to see a small deer stagger off into the ditch. Clint hit the breaks, while we gathered our thoughts and tried to figure out what to do. We were in the middle of nowhere with no cell service. Clint ran out to make sure she was still alive, and then we turned around and headed up an old dirt road we had just passed, in search of help.

There were a couple of older guys out sitting in the yard, so Clint got out of the van and filled them in. One of them got his hand gun (kept in a safety bag), jumped in the back with the boys, and we headed back to find Bambi. It was not lost on me, in the moment, how weird things had just gotten. The boys were stricken with silence, riding in the back of the van with a stranger holding a loaded handgun in his lap. I tried to make small talk to take the edge off; they must have been terrified. By the time we made it back, someone had called the local Sheriff about the commotion on the side of the road. We led them to Bambi and the Sheriff used his rifle to send her to heaven while we took photos, feeling terrible. We were instructed to stop at the next town and fill out an accident report, which we did, and were back on the road within an hour. Minutes later, we all got the giggles. I think it was a combination of stress release and remembering how crazy Clint had gotten behind the wheel, and none of us could stop laughing. Note to self, no more Starbucks Frappuccinos! He agreed. We crossed the border back into our homeland without incident, settled into our cheap roadside motel for the night, and ordered Chinese food. We had been living, eating, and sleeping in the van for weeks so I insisted we find a car wash and give it a good cleaning. The next day was July 1, Canada Day- how fitting! Our good friends in Kamloops were having a barbecue at 2:00 pm that we were trying to make it back for. We left very early for the seven-hour trip home. We gassed up the van and hit Tim Hortons for breakfast for the first time since Dubai. It was a true Canadian homecoming.

CHAPTER 20

Home

W
e made it to the barbecue on time! As much as I was dreading the return to reality and to the uncertainty of home, I couldn't have been more excited to see our friends. Some I had chatted with occasionally, but others I had literally not seen or talked to since we left almost eight months before. We surprised everyone by arriving on time and were greeted with excited hugs and millions of questions. Our plan was to spend two or three nights in Kamloops with our friends Chris and Julie, see whoever else we could, accomplish some business and banking errands, and then hit the road again heading northeast to Alberta. We would stop to see Clint's side of the family first, and then continue to Hinton for my Grandma's birthday party.

It was a whirlwind couple of days in Kamloops, but before we knew it we were loaded up in our home-away-from-home yet again. The boys stayed at Clint's sister Michelle's place while the two of us stayed with my mom and dad. We had family dinners and the cousins stayed up late and cruised around town together, all so excited to be together again. We even squeezed in a good old Canadian tradition and drove out to the rodeo grounds to watch the Chuckwagon races with my parents.

We had originally rented out our home on a year lease, which left us essentially homeless until October. This sounds potentially scary, however we were also jobless so the fewer bills we had piling up, the better. Having our house rented out meant that we at least had our financial bases covered.

I had put out a plea on Facebook for anyone leaving in the summer who might need a house-sitter, that we would be available and more than willing. I had heard back from a few friends already and we had our first few weeks lined up. It meant a lot of packing and unpacking over the next few months, but each home was already more or less familiar to us so it took the edge off of how exhausting it might end up being. In the end, we landed three different house-sits ranging from five days to three weeks long, and that took us to the end of August.

One night while we were at the local YMCA for a swim and a hot tub, Clint ran into Jeff, a close family friend that we hadn't seen yet since our return. Clint had been through a few job and business leads but as of yet, nothing had panned out. He mentioned that he had been on the hunt for work and Jeff told him to stop by his family's trucking shop. They had recently taken on a new tire business and thought Clint's experience with the tire industry might be valuable to them. He stopped by the next morning, had a meeting with the family, and they put him to work immediately. It was only meant to be casual, but as the days wore on, he eventually started working there full-time and we felt blessed beyond belief. It was physically hard work that he hadn't done since he was in his early 20's, but it was paying our bills and could hopefully be a foot in the door for something bigger down the pipe.

By the end of August, our house-sits were running out, the start of the school year was right around the corner, and we felt uncertain about where life would lead us. By now, I was ready for the boys to go to public school. It had never been my intention for them to homeschool right through to graduation, so it was time to register and choose courses for the fall. Rylan was about to begin Grade 7 and wasn't ready to go back to public school quite yet, but the other two were excited for the high school experience, so we registered them for Grades 9 and 10 and picked from the electives that still had space, which weren't many.

That same day we heard from an acquaintance who knew we were still looking for a place to stay and had a connection, so we made some calls and before nightfall had another six-week long house-sit lined up. That would take us right to the time we got back into our house. And we even got a puppy with this job! The boys could not have been more excited. God was so good and taking care of our every need. Carson jumped straight back into ice hockey, right where he had left off and continued the relationship with Kessa, the girl he'd been chatting with all year. We met her in person and figured out quite quickly that she was going to be more than just Carson's friend. School started well for all the kids, Clint was enjoying his job, and our house-sit turned out to be a perfect fit. We were back in our home city, settled, and our eleven-month trip around the world was about to become only a memory.

"So what was your favourite place?"

"Highlights? Lowlights?"

"Were you ever scared?"

"Best food?"

These and many similar questions were posed to us daily once we were back home in Canada, and no, it didn't get old. We all *loved* talking about our trip. 'Travel' had been replaced by couch-surfing, house-sitting, and many hours of visiting over coffee while we caught up with family and friends. Even while we had continued to bounce around from home to home and city to city, the kids easily settled into whatever routine was going on at the time. I eagerly welcomed the return of their upbeat personalities, once their comfort level returned to normal. The boys' badly missed relationships with their cousins were rekindled, and we treasured the time we had available to spend with people without a deadline to get back like we had pre-trip, when we had constantly faced the need to get home to work and home routines.

But coming home came with its own share of uncertainty. People were surprised to hear that Clint and I weren't exactly happy or ready to be home yet, even though the kids obviously were. It's bittersweet. Travelling had been hard—way harder than I imagined it would be in terms of constantly being challenged with life lessons or problems I needed to fix. The surprise to everyone was that it hadn't been hard in terms of missing our old life and that we had never longed to go home to it. The excitement of seeing and spending time with loved ones was shadowed by the fact that the freshness of the return would soon be gone and a new normal would set in. The adventure would be over and life would once again return to early mornings, overrun schedules, and working to live. Even though it was only early autumn, the air was thick with smoke, a reminder of the terrible forest fires that are part of life in western Canada, and the long, dark, cold of winter we always dread was only months away.

Our twentieth wedding anniversary arrived; an accomplishment in itself I would say! But if you told me ten years ago that we'd spend our twentieth anniversary career-less, homeless, and house-sitting for months, of course I wouldn't have believed you. I also wouldn't have believed that we'd have travelled around the world with our kids for nine months, so we definitely had no regrets! The dilemma we wrestled with now was wanting to give our kids everything they wanted in life, while neither of us really wanted to come home and do all of 'this' again. 'This' as in, the rat race, or 'the hamster wheel,' as Clint and I call it. Chasing the mighty dollar; working to live; attempting to afford even small luxuries in this extremely expensive country, while simultaneously trying to resist the pressure to 'keep up with the Joneses' at any cost. Reflecting on our conversation in the ocean in Mexico a month or two back, *had we really asked each other all the hard questions?* The money sunk into equity in our home would go a lot farther if we lived somewhere cheaper, if we had the courage to live a different kind of life. *Ouch!* Ouch, because with kids happily content with a first-world life, planted in childhood friendships and good youth groups and the desire to pursue sports, how on earth could we up and leave it all? I have no answer except that we couldn't, at least not yet. We had decided together to come back and get jobs or buy a business and pray for a least a little more freedom than we had yet found in any job or business in the last twenty years.

For the sake of our kids, we decided to plug back in to life and attempt to choose joy. We thanked God for health and family and that our many friends seemed overjoyed to have us back. We had a home in a city that we do actually enjoy and appreciate, a loving church family; so for the sake of our kids, we decided to plug back in to life and attempt to choose joy. We had a home in a city that we do actually enjoy and appreciate, a loving church family; so much to look forward to. In the meantime we'd savour the travels we'd already been blessed with, scour expat travel groups, and bookmark international living websites with hope in our hearts. Maybe a future season of our life would bring us exactly the life we dream of. For now, we had work to do!

CHAPTER 21

What Now?

As a mother, I started feeling better as the kids settled back in and we all found our groove again. For the most part, our family just picked up where we'd left off as members of our community. But I was also feeling more restless than ever, processing questions that our experience left me with, and figuring out how to move forward. *How does one see the world, wake up in a new destination on a weekly basis, eat exciting and interesting foreign foods, meet new people every day, always have something to look forward to, and then just settle?* I perused our photos nightly, remembering every sight, smell and flavour as if we were just there, experiencing it all over again in my mind. I tried bringing up fun memories at the dinner table; sometimes my family obliged and sometimes the conversation moved swiftly to something else. I was sadly yearning for what the trip had been and having difficulty accepting that it was all over. Our church culture had changed somehow— or maybe we had, it was hard to tell. We didn't feel like we fit in anymore and were having trouble connecting with old friends. *How do I possibly sit and have coffee with someone and just discuss the weather or share gossip when I've ridden a camel and snorkelled the Great Barrier Reef?* Occasionally someone would want to hear a story or two, but it quickly became old news to people. By mid-September I went to work putting together a 100-page coffee table photo-book of our grand adventure in full-colour. Every night I sat at my computer and collected our photos together into collaged themes and designs unique to each country. By the end I had somehow compiled over 3,500 photos into 350 of our most favourite and precious memories. I could not have been more overjoyed the day it arrived in my mailbox. It had been the perfect way to dream again, even if only for a few weeks.

By the end of September, it was clear that my mental health was taking a hit and my physical health was in sharp decline. I felt anxious to the high heavens over nothing all the time, and my heart was always racing which ran contrary to the fact that I could easily sleep the day away. Between school and sports and church, we were already drastically over-scheduled and I was feeling it. I was down and needed to pick myself back up again. Life had to go on. So I booked an appointment with a new naturopath and after some bloodwork and testing, was put on a great treatment plan for my thyroid and adrenals. We moved home mid-October. The boys coming home again after leaving that house almost a year earlier, were all inches taller now, and had completely grown out of all the clothes and belongings that we had left behind. We purged like we had never purged before and started fresh. Carson came to us one day and apologized for how he had behaved on the trip. It hadn't taken him much more than five minutes back in Kamloops to see that nothing had changed and he hadn't missed out on anything. He was regretting his anger and pouting and felt terrible for his behaviour. We forgave him and moved on. It was a welcome relief to hear him reflect and take responsibility.

I took pleasure in displaying my souvenir magnet collection, reminders of the countries we had visited, on the front of my fridge door. Every time I went for milk or eggs, it was pure joy to be reminded about our time in Amsterdam or Dubai. They weren't just frivolous experiences after all. They were life lessons that we were still learning long after we returned home. We learned how to carve a pineapple and drive on the "wrong" side of the road in Fiji. We learned what a cuppa (cup of coffee) and a brolly (umbrella) were in Australia, and how not to get scammed in Thailand. I learned to respect Muslim culture and cover my shoulders in Oman, and in Israel we learned that the world still had a lot to learn about Jesus. We learned about greek mythology in Greece, and in Italy we learned that if you book an overnight train you'll miss the scenery. In Germany we learned about the Holocaust and that speed limits are overrated and unnecessary. Amsterdam taught us more than we cared to know about the red light district, and that we are far too old to enjoy overnight busses. In Scotland and London we were reminded how young of a country Canada is by comparison to the majority of the world. In Wales we learned that good friends are hard to come by, so hold dear to the ones that do. We learned how to relax and master the cliff jump in Mexico. There, too, I learned that I love fresh papaya, and that when you love God, you love his people, and that they are family everywhere. We learned how to surf sand dunes in New Mexico, and the history of the dinosaur in Utah. I also learned to take a time out when I need one, and also that it is *okay* to need one. The boys learned how to navigate airports and city maps and how to pay attention to where they are going in case they get lost coming home. We all learned how to budget, and live minimally, and that stuff and things are fleeting but experiences last a lifetime.

That's all we had, experiences that became memories. Sometimes they surfaced in conversation and sometimes they didn't. We may never understand the magnitude of such an adventure together, the lasting effects of so many months in close proximity, the frustrating and emotional times, the laughter and the fear. We grew and were challenged and we all changed in more ways than one. *Returning home isn't the end*, I told myself. *In many ways it's just the beginning.* We still have a lot of the world to see and nothing but time. I have no doubt that we aren't finished scratching our travel itch; the seed has merely been planted. I thank God every day for this experience and for allowing this dream in my heart to come to fruition. We wound up where we were supposed to be for the new season and I woke up each morning and was okay with that.....or at least I tried. In the meantime, I had a book to write. My memories became a memoir, and the images and experiences alive in my mind became a story.

I hope I've inspired you, the reader, in some way or another. Life is short and you only live once. The world is waiting to be seen, touched, tasted and heard. Get out and get to know her. I'm sure glad that I did.

EPILOGUE

Two words… Covid 19. It's May 2020 as I write this, and the global pandemic has set in.

I was inspired to start writing almost immediately upon moving back into our house in October 2017. I stayed up late many times, writing long into the night when it was quiet, when I could think without disruption. I got about as far as Thailand and then petered out. I'd pick up where I left off a few times over the three years, but always fell flat and could never seem to carve out time to get it finished. And then the shot heard around the world… Covid 19 changed everything.

After working for our friend Jeff for a few months, the opportunity to invest in a downtown mechanic shop was presented to Clint and we gladly accepted. It was an older shop, but we had big plans to incorporate some new machinery and services, so we went in 50/50 with a partner and on January 1, 2018 we became the new owners. It's been 2 ½ years now, and business is great. Clint has worked hard and built the shop up tremendously. We look forward to a few more years in business-building mode and then we'll see where the wind takes us. He's still golfing in his spare time and enjoying his return to the business world. He calls these his "money-makin' years!"

Carson went to public school for the first part of Grade 10 and decided it wasn't a great fit for him. He was eager to graduate early and felt that online school would provide him with a better and easier opportunity to complete high school faster so he came home after one semester. He worked hard day and night, finishing school, playing rep hockey, and working two jobs. He saved enough for a car and in two quick years graduated in May of 2019. He has taken a year off of study while he works and saves for school. He intends to try out and hopefully play hockey at Liberty University in Virginia in the fall. His friendship with Kessa turned into a full-blown romance to no surprise of ours, and almost three years later they are still happily together and recently engaged! She graduated from the same online school and class as Carson, which made it an even more special occasion as we were able to celebrate with her and her family. He plans on studying business with a major in accounting or architectural engineering. His foray into the working world has changed his outlook on life quite a bit, and as karma would have it, all Kessa wants to do is travel! God really does have a sense of humour.

Braden went back to public school for Grade nine and did great, but also realized it might not be the best fit for him either. He attended online school for Grade 10, and until his second semester of Grade 11. At that point he was frustrated and overwhelmed with the work-load and we collectively decided it was time for him to give our local private Christian school a try. He was back successfully for one whole month when Covid hit and he's been home and back online again ever since, much to all of our dismay. Outside of school, he's almost 17, thriving and well-adjusted with lots of friends, and although our relationship with him tends to need a little more effort than the other two boys, it is healthy. He still loves soccer and just recently picked up golf, much to Clint's excitement. His memories of our trip are a mixed bag, but overall he would speak highly of it and is excited to travel in the future.

Rylan is 15, in Grade 9, and transitioned from homeschooling to online school this year. It has been a better fit for both of us and he seems to be doing well, but our plans are for him to go to the Christian school with Braden next year and to graduate there. He also returned to playing ice hockey, and I guess it's ok to credit Covid with his new love of downhill biking. He has a solid group of four or five meaningful long-term friendships with guys that he plays hockey and bikes with. He is still by far the quietest and hardest to read. He keeps his feelings in check and holds his cards close to his chest.

I do the books for the business from home and just recently went back to work (after 18 years at home) at a big-box retail store. With the boys back at school, it was time for me to experiment with returning to work. It was short-lived, again because of Covid, but it was fun while it lasted and a great new experience. This pause in life freed up my time to get back to writing and finishing the story of our grand adventure. I've been writing many hours each day, and late into the nights again. Reflecting has been so rewarding. I use Facebook to look back and remind myself of details such as hotel names, and I lose time sorting through photos, remembering all the sights and sounds of our amazing time together.

The fall after we returned home, we took a family trip to Florida for ten glorious days (minus Carson who was working and playing hockey.) We spent half of our time in Orlando and then the other half exploring the Keys. Clint and I took a couple's trip to Texas last fall to see friends, and we took likely one of our last full-family vacations last summer to Atlantic Canada. We arrived in Halifax and spent three days in the area before venturing to the amazing and charming Prince Edward Island. We rented a Jeep for the trip and spent our time beach combing, golfing, hiking, and biking. Our return home included a very long layover in Toronto, Ontario, so in typical planning fashion, I took that opportunity to book us in for a day trip to the majestic Niagara Falls!

Covid has us bound to Canada this summer, but we've maximized the time exploring our own neck of the woods instead of heading south like we usually do. Just last weekend we met family in Jasper National Park, and I have two more weekends booked, one in Sun Peaks, BC and another doing a fun hot springs tour at the end of August. I also recently took a gamble and booked Christmas in Jamaica, fingers crossed and prayers going up that this amazing trip will happen! Braden's Grade 12 class has a trip planned to Peru which I plan to chaperone and we have good friends that just recently moved to Spain, so we should be soon figuring out when we'll make it there.

As you can see, we have no plans to settle down. Travel will always be a huge part of our life. Whenever I'm not making an actual plan, I'm researching exciting places to go. We keep our possessions to a minimum, carry zero debt, and I save every extra penny to put towards trips, either abroad or road trips closer to home. It's an exciting time to be alive and we love our life and try to live it to the fullest. Thanks for tagging along for the ride and thanks for reading. I hope we've inspired you!

Fun Facts

8 months

16 countries

9 states

56 accommodations

49 free nights on credit card points

5 national parks

7 flights

20,000 kms driving

5 rental cars

2 overnight trains

1 16-day cruise

1 overnight ferry

1 overnight bus

3439 photos

Favourite	Least Favourite Destination
Shauna- #1 Greece #2 Australia	Least- didn't have one
Clint- #1 Australia	Least- didn't have one
Carson- #1 Dubai #2 Australia	Least- Fiji
Braden- #1 Australia	Least- Amsterdam
Rylan- #1 Dubai	Least- Fiji

Favourite Food

Shauna- Chicken Schnitzel, beer battered fries and Custard Slice-Australia ~ Khao Soy Noodles-Thailand

Clint-Massaman Curry and mango sticky rice-Thailand

Carson- Crepes and smoothies-Thailand and McSpiders (Coke/Ice cream float)-Australia

Braden- McSpiders-Australia, Crepes and Smoothies-Thailand

Rylan-Pineapple Fried Rice-Thailand and Crepes and Smoothies-Thailand

Favourite Memory

Shauna-Hillsong Church and WhiteHaven Beach Australia, Wales with the Kerrigans

Clinton- Christmas in Australia, St. Andrews Scotland, The Burj Dubai

Carson- The sand dunes and desert adventure in Dubai and Christmas in Australia

Braden-Cliff Jumping and Cenotes/Mexico, The Burj/Dubai, Family time/Australia

Rylan-Christmas and Dreamworld with the cousins in Australia, Cliff Jumping/Mexico

ABOUT THE AUTHOR

Shauna lives in Kamloops, BC Canada with her husband of 23 years, and three sons aged 19, 17 and 16, and her beloved mini aussie-doodle Mylo. She homeschooled her boys for ten years, does the books for the family's businesses part time and has multiple side hustles which she uses to save money in her travel fund. She can now scratch "travel around the world" off of her bucket list but still aspires to see and do so much more! She loves Jesus, coffee with cream and sugar, movies, reading, baking, foreign foods, and travel. She loves and misses the beach and vows to live closer to it one day.

Made in the USA
Monee, IL
04 December 2021